THIRSTING FOR PEACE IN A RAGING CENTURY

## Among Edward Sanders Books

Poem from Jail (1963)

Peace Eye (1966)

The Family: The Manson Group and Aftermath (1971, Updates 1990, 2002)

Egyptian Hieroglyphics (1973)

Tales of Beatnik Glory, Volume I (1975)

Investigative Poetry (1976)

20,000 A.D. (1976)

Fame & Love in New York (1980)

The Z-D Generation (1981)

Thirsting for Peace in a Raging Century: Selected Poems 1961–1985 (1987)

Tales of Beatnik Glory, Volumes I & 2 (1990)

Hymn to the Rebel Cafe—Poems 1986-1991 (1993)

Chekhov: A Biography in Verse (1995)

1968: A History in Verse (1997)

The Poetry and Life of Allen Ginsberg (2000)

America: A History in Verse: Volume 1. 1900-1939 (2000)

Volume 2. 1940-1961 (2000)

Volume 3. 1962-1970 (2004)

Tales of Beatnik Glory Vols. 1–4 (2004)

Poems for New Orleans (2008)

America, a History in Verse, the Twentieth Century, CD edition (2009)

Let's Not Keep Fighting the Trojan War: New and Selected Poems 1986–2009

## Recent Chapbooks

Stanzas for Social Change (2005)

This Morning's Joy (2008)

Revs of the Morrow (2008)

## CDs

Sanders Truckstop (1970)

Beer Cans on the Moon (1972)

Songs in Ancient Greek (1988)

American Bard (1995)

Thirsting for Peace (2005)

Poems for New Orleans (with Mark Bingham) (2007)

# THIRSTING FOR PEACE IN A RAGING CENTURY

SELECTED POEMS 1961–1985

## Edward Sanders

NEW AND REVISED EDITION

COFFEE HOUSE PRESS : : MINNEAPOLIS : : 2009

Coffee House Press books are available to the trade through our primary distributor, Consortium Book Sales & Distribution, www.cbsd.com. For personal orders, catalogs, or other information, write to: Coffee House Press, 79 Thirteenth Avenue NE, Suite 110, Minneapolis, MN 55413.

Coffee House Press is a nonprofit literary publishing house. Support from private foundations, corporate giving programs, government programs, and generous individuals helps make the publication of our books possible. We gratefully acknowledge their support in detail in the back of this book.

Good books are brewing at coffeehousepress.org

LIBRARY OF CONGRESS CATALOGING-IN-PUBLICATION DATA
Sanders, Ed.
Thirsting for peace in a raging century : selected poems, 1961–1985
Edward Sanders. — New and rev. ed.
p. cm.
ISBN 978-1-56689-238-4 (alk. paper)
I. Title.
PS3569.A49T5 2009
811'.54—dc22
2009028061
PRINTED IN THE UNITED STATES
10 9 8 7 6 5 4 3 2 1
FIRST REVISED EDITION | FIRST PRINTING

ACKNOWLEDGMENTS: Some of the poems in this book were published in the following magazines: Fuck you/ A Magazine of the Arts, The World, Sulfur, City Lights Review, Paris Review, Crawdaddy, The Folklore Center newsletter, The Los Angeles Free Press, Earth's Daughters, Pearl, Light Work, Fathar, Yanagi, The Portable Lower East Side, and Woodstock Times.

Some of these poems appeared in the following anthologies: All Stars (Viking Grossman), The Post Moderns:New American Poetry Revisited (Grove), Anthology Of New York Poets (Random House), New Writing In The U.S.A. (Penguin), The Rag and Bone Shop of the Heart (HarperCollins), Civil Disobedience: Poetics And Politics In Action (Coffee House), The Paris Review Anthology (Norton), Up Late— American Poetry Since 1970 (4Walls 8 Windows), Out Of This World (Crown).

Some of these poems appeared in the following books: Peace Eye (Frontier Press), Egyptian Hieroglyphics (Institute for Further Studies), 20,000 A.D. (North Atlantic Books), Investigative Poetry (City Lights), Hymn To Maple Syrup (P.C.C. Publications), The Cutting Prow (Am/Here Books), Hymn to the Rebel Café (Black Sparrow), Cracks Of Grace (Woodland Pattern), Stanzas For Social Change (Shivastan), The Z/D Generation (Station Hill).

And some of these poems appeared in a few other publications whose names have been lost by the author during these moiling decades. He apologizes.

*For my mentors, Allen Ginsberg and Charles Olson,*
*and for the friendship of fellow poets such as*
*Michael McClure, Ted Berrigan, Duncan McNaughton,*
*Joanne Kyger, d.a. levy, Diane di Prima, Gary Snyder,*
*Lawrence Ferlinghetti, Bob Holman, Robert Bly, Phil Whalen,*
*Tom Clark, Ron Padgett, Anne Waldman, and many others*

## Adios Diamond Sutra

## Egyptian Hieroglyphs

## Why Hesitate to Know All Gentle Things

## In di Gasn, tsu di Masn

# Protest and Survive

# Poem from Jail

—writing paper was not allowed
at the Montville State Jail, in
Uncasville, Connecticut, where the author
resided August 8-24, 1961 on a charge
of attempting to swim aboard a Polaris
submarine in a peace demonstration,
so this poem was created on the insides
of cigarette packs and scrolls of toilet paper,
then smuggled out in his shoe.


I.

Redeem Zion!
Stomp up over
the Mountain!

To live as "beatific
Spirits welded
                together,"
To live with
        a fierce pacifism,
To love in haste,
as a beetle
entering bark,

To dance with
flaming mane,

All these, a man,
I, steaming, proud
have sought
as a harlot
her jewels & paint,
as belly seeks out
belly;

And we have
demanded that
they ban the bomb,
mouth of death
convulsing upon the earth,
and the bomb gores
the guts of earth
like a split-nail
in a foot fetish,
and the salt domes
rumble
as the arse
of a politician,
and Nevada
is a kangaroo
with its pouch
chopped open
by the AEC;

And at my ear
was the whirr
of wings,
"red wing,
black wing,
black wing
        shot with crimson,"
and the Bird-Flock
stared to my eye,
and always the Birds
flap overhead
        shrieking
        like a "berserk
        tobacco auction":
Pains! Neverbirth! Dieness!

And we have
seen the failure
of Stassen
and the Teller
intervention

& Radford
in there wailing,
also,
for Death.*

And Madame
Chiang Kai-Shek
too old now
to fuck for the
          China Lobby,

And we have learned
the Hidden History
of the Korean War,
and MacArthur
who retreated
               before
non-existent
Chinese Hordes,

And we have seen denied
Mao's creation,
And we have denied
Van Gogh's Crow
shrieking on the
               horizon,
and Rouault's Jesus.

Chant        Chant
             O American!
lift up the Stele
             anti    bomb;
O American
             is there
an Eagle of Pacifism?
             Is there
a bevy of symbolic
             Birds?

* See I. F. Stone's book, *The Hidden History of the Korean War.*

The Rot Bird,
             The Claw Hawk,
The Sexy Dove,
             The Cormorant
                      of Oceanus,
The Sea-Crow
             of bloody claws,
Pigeon of the dance
      of the belly,

             Birds
             Birds
Shrieks and furry assemblage
             Birds
             Birds
Blurred birds in flight
             Birds
             Birds
Da Vinci's tail feathers,
      Dream of Youth
             Birds
             Birds
Ginsberg's birds Ginsberg's
sacred scroll to Naomi
Birds of the fluttering eyes,
             Birds never asleep
             diaphanous eyelids.

Between the
Bevy of Birds
& the Sexy Lamb
there is nothing Else.

The Father negative
The Son negative
The Holy Ghost negative.

      Aphrodite
      Kallipugos
      remains, the

hieroglyphs remain,
    "Trees die
        but the Dream
        remains"
Van Gogh & Ginsberg,
The Burning Bush,
The Trembling Flank,
        All remain.
Anubis & the
                power of Amulets,
The Beetle of Endlessness,
                they remain.
My flesh abides.
My electrical meat
        chatters for
a wink of eternity
between dark cunt
        and the grave.


        II.


Trembling     Trembling
murderous flank
of Now,

Napoleon
        is Now
& was
        and shall,
Napoleon
    stomping all
    over Europe; &
Europa has an
older meaning,

    Europa fucked
    for centuries
    by the Bull of Zeus;
    &
    Pasiphaë

Pasiphaë, also,
what contortions
had you
to writhe thru
to receive
the prick
of the Bull!
you O Pasiphaë
inside the
sacred cow-skin
of Crete,
as the long tool
of the Bull arched
and gored its way
into your snatch,
O Pasiphaë
what thrill
& thunder
you felt,
& what nutty
offspring,
ah the Karma
of that fuck;

"No man who has spent
a month in the death cells
believes in capital punishment

No man who has spent
a month in the death cells
believes in cages for beasts"

No man.
        fucking in the sheaves,
        leaping in the aether,
        lusting for the sun,
        I, a man, my skull
        lined with bird-roosts,
        a man, disjunctive
        coalescence of thoughts,

trembly, bristling,
tense beyond belief,
wandering, relating
thing to thing,
balling the All,
hands twisting in
       Moistness,
heart bubbling in
       Vasthood,
eyes bouncing to th'
       Glaze,
brain puking in th'
       Word-stream,
legs sucked in to
       Oceanus.

Anubis grins slyly
at the dock,
O American,
O Traveler.
The Sun-boat
enters the Vastness,
Anubis stomps
with the Sun-shafts,
& the sun awaits,
the sun, the
eye of the
Trembling Lamb.
Move onward
O Traveler
of thick sandals
& matted hair,
flouting your
choice-patterns,
for you shall
enter the
Mountain,
& the warmth
of the living
darkness, the

warmth as the warmth
between bellies,
& the closeness
as the closeness
                there.
Carve a staff
traveler, carve
it with the days,
notch it with
the ways and paths,
in the journey,
under the corn-furrow,
where Persephone
is ravished by
her gloom lover,
Dis, Pluto,
& Persephone is Darkness
also;

You shall Enter,
Traveler,
   in the myriad
directions of the
            prepositions,

            & bounce in
            & bounce over
The Trembling Flank

            & enter in
            & enter over
The Sexy Lamb
            & shriek in
            & shriek over
The Sun-shafts
            and Sun-barge.

III.

And I have crawled
through the forest
near the Doom's Day Machine,
puking blood
& clutching guts,
And I have clutched
my Amulet, Ammonite,
for dreams,
& have used
my sacred slab
Of Voidal Concretions
as pillow
& have clutched
my scrolls,
& have held
the covenant of my mind
and certain artifacts,
as sacred,
and have notched
my staff with
the times,
& have clothed
the body with
feathers from
the Bevy of Birds,
& my arms thrust
themselves out
of feathers,
prick dangles
out of feathers,
head barfs itself
out of feathers;
on my feet are
sandals,
in my heart
is a ravenous Duck;
& I have laid bare
my choice-patterns,

freaked in the
shit of Being,
& I am laid
bare in the
  Burning Bush,
& have pissed
out of the holly leaves
& my whiteness
is as the
whiteness of the Lamb.

And we have
seen the men
farting around
in Geneva,
and the governments
have not clasped
one another
as lovers,
shedding the
buffer-zones,
confronting
each other
in Nakedness.

No, they have
not halted hate.
Yes, it is true;
Death shall assume
the continuum.
If I am turned
to atomic death
here in my cell,
let me leave behind
for earthologists
a masturbation,
love-body of
continuing
nonviolence;
and I shall

project myself
to that time
where I am
clad in feathers,
& my mind
is ejaculated
into the Cosmos,
& I breathe
the god-breath,
& dance
in the rays
of Nonviolence,
staring into forever.


IV.


Whom
do we blame
as we stomp
upstage    downstage
left-center
            right-center,
beaming
         in the wings,
balling
            in the orchestra;
Whom do we
blame, O Traveler,
in your journey
thru the
thighs of Cosmos,

    O Traveler
let us blame
the cowardly,
& those in charge
of money,
the economists
& the profiteers,

and the hidden
men in the
military,
& all those who
profit by Death,

And let us place blame
upon
"the enormous
organized cowardice."

O Zeus
may I come forth
bearing a vase & cakes
in the presence
of the gods

may I walk
by the side of my lake
every day
without ceasing

& may I stand
in a perpetual tremble
near the rock-pool

and may the waters
bear back
a reflection
        in godhead

may pierce my face
into the way
of darkness

may I receive offerings
in the underworld
with the flowers
crescent
on the dock
of Lethe

may I build then
my tomb
& may I go out
in triumph,
O Zeus
Great-grandson
of the earth,
O Zeus,
third generation
from Chaos,
O Zeus,
grand-nephew
of the
Spectres of Vengeance!*

Morphelized
motherfucking
            badfaithed
pukelips of a
hesitant puker!
Puke dropping to
a bottomless pit!
sore of a thousand
pustules!
mammary
spitting out
clabber!
mono-archal
desensitized demon
vaunting
anti-love!
septic excrescence
cut in lozenges!
Endless flypaper,
barrier between
bellies,
hater &

---

* On the genealogy of Zeus, and its various possibilities,
  see Hesiod's *Theogony*, lines 1–117.

desensitizer
that lies down
between
the bride
    and bridegroom,
Paper cup that
expands to
an incredible
Vastness!
Steel that slits
the throat of
the Sexual Lamb,
Buttocks
with a painted face
and a tongue sticking
out the asshole!

. . . . . . O Jesus!
am I howling
at my country again,
America of the
United States,
where the
new Now culture
is balling its
way toward
the pluperfection.
America which
is th' only
choice left
and place
for the great
  Goof City.

v.

Do, nipple
of wet-nurse,
cascade,

in chant time,
cascade,
voice behind
the Waterfall
    of Whiteness,
nipple that
dropped on me,
moist &
budded, beautiful,
fully & yielding,
nipple,
butterfly
on a white mountain,
and the body
behind breast
rocking,
and the voice
behind breast
singing,
and the warmth
there
beyond belief;
cascade,
nipple bursting
out of brightness;
and the cunning
be there, also,
of the wetnurse
as she played
with me,
there in the
half-light,
and the breast
lowered from above,
and she bubbled
the milk
on to her hand
and I licked
from there
which I shall

never forget,
& shall never cease
from sensing;
wet-nurse
unhooking brassiere,
then brassiere
in disarray
& breasts
dropping from under
the whiteness of cloth;
Vastness dangling
           in Vastness,
light
cascading
among shadows;
breasts laid softly,
touching
cheek and eye,
eye never to forget,
never,
though the memory
be tattered
and the mind
be shredded.

VI.

Goof City,
Infinite cock
& granite snatch,
& whiteness
as almond
out of the husk,
& strange sounds
           There,
temple of
Aphrodite
Kallipugos,

O City
"whose Terraces
are the color
of stars,"

your monuments
the reflection
of crystal,

O City,
thou art beautiful
as the rubies
in thy women's
navels,

thou art as
carefully painted
as thy dancers,

The blueness of
your water
is as a
tinted eyelid,

you are a
nipple
on a mountain,

your streets
are as cross-cords
over belly flesh,

your gates
are as parted lips;

Goof City,
where every choice
is allowed,
        Goof City,
the city of the
Trembling Flank,

Smile & Crotch
without fester,

City without
the Great Cancer

& Cancer not
worshiped
on its Altars,

nor bloated motion,

Goof City,
laughter
laugher
and flaming Teeth.


VII.


"The Doomsday Machine. A Doomsday Weapon System might
hypothetically be described as follows: Let us assume that for 10
billion dollars one could build a device whose function is to
destroy the earth. This device is protected from enemy action
(perhaps by being situated thousands of feet underground) and
then connected to a computer, in turn connected to thousands of
sensory devices all over the United States. The computer would
be programmed so that if, say, five nuclear bombs exploded over
the United States, the device would be triggered and the earth
destroyed." —Herman Kahn

And the "Case"
for disarmament
was read &
chewed up
in the mind.
And as I
sped by
I wanted to
explain

the Birds I found
in, on, around,
myself
when I looked, &
the Theory of Anubis,
The Trembling Flank,
The Sexual Lamb,
The Amulet of Ammonite,
The Beetle,
All these,
as I sped past
and spent the life
perfecting
Orgasm.
Yes, I
was a fuck-
ing Unilateralist,
& was
walking among th'
Machinery,
& stood at
the closure
where the
Doom's Day Box
sucks in its data
from the air,
and was a
stave of flesh
among reeds of metal,
and the voice,
the mind's-lance
out of the mouth,
blended with metal noise,
as a trill commixed
in the tinkle
of reeds;
and I loved
to walk in Machinery
& stroke the
Antennae

pronged out of
the soil,
& mixed my voice
in the din There:
Hate is a murrain!

Krrrr
from the Machine

Fuck off, Death Machine!

Krrrtlelinnnnq
from the Doom box

Death Metal!!

Krrrrrrrrrr,
and I
was coughing Thoreau
at them
in my
Civil
Disobedience
in that forest
where the
Doom's Day Machine
lay buried,
projecting its
death Antennae
in the air;
& I walked
and wailed
The Machine
be placed
under U.N. control;
& remained there,
wailing,
till they programmed
the Doom's Day Box
against

Trespassers;
And it came to pass
that each pacifist foot
in the hallowed
inclosure
was a trigger,
And I
consulted
the magic
to create an
implosion
of Love
to balance th'
explosion
of Hate
there.

But all I made
was a mild
Aphrodisiac
& set loose
some platonic vapors;

And then stood
in the Forest,
howling by megaphone
at the Closure,
and they pro-
grammed the Doom's
Day Machine
against picketing
also,
& the Moan
of the epilept
passed my teeth,
& my Eye
before the claws
of the Rot Bird
was as a dead horse
under a vulture,

and my Eye
was dancing
freak-beams
on itself,
& my mind
was as a feed-bowl
in the flash
of bird claws,
& I strode
to the desert,
& walked the roads,
& fell to a
crawl,
onward,
bloody glaze
bloody tongue
bloody hands.


VIII.

to
flip was to flip
like the Spiral
Galaxy,
Brain slain in the
word-stream,
& the arms
were crooked up
to ward off Void,
and my heart
was as a bird
buffed up
to a wall
in the wind;

The road
twisted
like a knife
across the desert

& slashed
    the throat
of Mountains,
& I crawled,
onward,
clutching guts
and coughing blood,
scrawling poems
on rocks
with a charred log
& laughing
to watch
a desert burst
wash out
the lines;
and crawled
all onward,
& entered the
Mountain,
Yes! crawled in
to the vastness,
crawled in
to squirm it out
with the
Grand Machine!
the lights descend
into the Darkness;
Demeter is roused
        out
by my Entrance,
& the ravening Lovers,
Dis and Persephone,
scream Darkness;
lamp-glares
float in the Black;
Brightness
is thrown back
as a glare
from beads
    of sweat.

IX.

Overflow
from an end-
less bedpan,
Mind oozing to
the outerstice,
& I have Entered,
eruptum spiritus,
downward, by
the shriekway,
downward;
& the man, me,
stomped into the
flip-stream; and th'
tears, outpukes,
inflips, cellular rot,
the eyes eyes balling
in the flip-stream
ears ears sucking
in the Vasthood
mind mind in the
Tremble-drama
heart heart merely
a relay station
brain brain slain
over Goof City;
these are the words
and this
is the man,
Mind behaving
like a berserk
foot fetish,
brainvalves torn
in the world-stream,
brain balling
the outerstice;
The Milky Way is a meeting of Maenads,
Floodlights stagger
the sunflower,

flowers jerk off
in infinity;

Bristling in the
bat-black,
mind spews out
to Nebulae;
   balling the All;
Darkness; swiveled
   into the Mountain;
Shriek it All!!
   Wand waved
over the thigh!
Sucked to the
Vortex,
Universal Hole,
Vastness,
clutching my Amulet,
Ammonite for dreams;
I spew
down thru the
mountain;
gone, flipped to
the reservoir,
dark lone
into the dark
to stomp it out
with the Metal Queen.

Moon wraps its legs around the earth,
Birds perch on a trellis of air,
Eye is the Rot Bird.
Heart is the Claw Hawk,
Crotch is in the Pelican.

# Leaflet for the Exorcism of the Pentagon

LEAFLET PREPARED FOR EXORCISM AND LEVITATION DEMONSTRATION
HELD AT THE PENTAGON, OCTOBER 1967

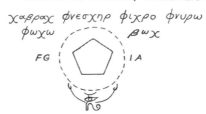

a magic rite to
exorcize the Spirits of murder,
violence & creephood
from the Pentagon.

1. purification rites for participants. cleansing
   of eye-heart-minds with Hittite spell

2. prayer for the soldiers & their violent karma
   in vietnam

3. consecration of the four directions

4. creation of magic circle for the
   protection of the rites. pouring of
   corn-meal trail about the pentagon

5. invocation of Powers & Spirits
   of exorcism

6. placing of love-articles & clothing onto
   the pentagon: beads, feathers, rock & roll records,
   books & the sacred Grope Relic.

7. ceremony of exorcism:

   EARTH -- physical contact with the pentagon

   AIR   -- conjuring of Malevolent Creep Powers

   WATER -- cleansing by liquid

   FIRE  -- destruction by fire

8. the rising of the pentagon

9. The EXORGASM! Banishment of the
               evil spirit. singing
               & shrieking

10. peace mantra.


This is the purification spell:

a-ri-ia-ad-da-li-is   Dim-an-za sar-ri ka-si-i
hu-u-e-hu-u-i-ia tap-pa-as-sa-it sar-ri ti-ia-mi
               hu-i-hu-i-ia

# I Am Creighton C. Blackmarket

*—from a demonstration in 1972*

I am General Creighton C. Blackmarket
I rip into the legs of villagers

       with tiny plastic bombs
     dropped from helicopters
   and robot platforms
          hovering above the jungles

I am defoliation     I am hideous scars     I am mothers
     keening in rubble.

     I am piles of stolen hardware
             on the blackmarket
                 Saigon waterfront

   stolen from the mouths
   of the poor

I am General Creighton C. Blackmarket
I bomb North Vietnam without
the approval of civilian authorities

I AM Gen. Creighton C. TERROR

I swoop down,
belching with fragmentation
bombs, lips flecked
with ghoul-drool,

                    upon the
                    soul of
                        America

I am the military-industrial-heroin complex
            I AM HEROIN
                    in grade schools
                    brought here by corrupt
                    U.S. officials in Southeast Asia

    I am the
    wheel of death
    spinning through
    the minds of the young

bearing heroin, racism, sexism, napalm, & fascism

            @@@@@@@@@@@@@@@@
              @@@@@@@@@
                @@@
                  @

# Universal Rent Strike Rag

*—a poem performed on my album*
Beer Cans on the Moon

When the last grim government is gone, my friend
And the last landlord is through
And the last policeman has thrown away his gun
And the last wire tap is done

And the Legions of Green are walking along
                         with their plastic shillelaghs held high
And the last computer has computed its last
                       and the Flags of Fantasy fly!

Oh birth, death, sex, gossip, politics, religion
Oh sing that Universal Rent Strike Rag
Not going to be anything left to do
But that Universal Rent Strike Rag!

When the plastic plexidomes are built on the moon
Socialist algae tanks are turning out cream
We'll sit by the banks of the hydroponic stream
And cackle and chortle in the Universal Dream

The last police state falls on the floor
Clothes are free at the dry goods store
The last hungry stomach is feasted full
The only thing left to talk about more

Is birth, death, sex, gossip, politics, religion
Sing that Universal Rent Strike Rag
There's not going to be anything left to do
But that Universal Rent Strike Rag.

## Homage to Love-Zap

*—for Judith Malina and Julian Beck*


I know that the robot
is struggling to form itself

    to chew into death
    the leaves of the rose.

I know with my soul-eye, the spirit of the fascist sewer
tries with its might

    to teach all mammals
    to live as garbage—

so that the muscleless lumps
    lie down in the metal cans
    & beg for the lids to be lowered.

 I know that it is useless
 yet with my last breath
 I shriek  I raise my fist
 I shout showers of love-bursts above the
         golf carts
 I violate the dictates of the werewolf freaks of war
 I circle up with lover friends
 to drive to distraction the uncreative circuits
 of the robot fists.
 Every day is May Day when you dance the dance.

Things line up to block
the molecules of my imagination
but I just add them to the frantic clutter!

Come o love-zap
Come of thrilling never-seen
    imaginations

Come and take me 'pon thy thrilling rides!
Come and take me
Come on come on come on

# The 12 Commandments

for the FBI, the CIA, and the Service Intelligence Agencies
—*to the memory of Senator Frank Church*

  1.  Thou shalt not kill our leaders
  2.  Thou shalt not break into our homes
  3.  Thou shalt not intercede against our meetings
  4.  Thou shalt not use poisons, germs, or toxins
  5.  Thou shalt not bug our offices and bedrooms
  6.  Thou shalt not break open our mail
  7.  Thou shalt not surveill us while we journey
  8.  Thou shalt not write false reports about us
  9.  Thou shalt not send provocateurs among us
10.  Thou shalt not use us to justify thy power
11.  Thou shalt not send spores of death among us
12.  Thou shalt not use drugs, hypnosis, robo-wash,
          behavior modification, or desensitization
              procedures to wire up thine agents

—1976
written in a time of
Genuine Reform

# Cemetery Hill

*—for Mollie Cravens Sanders*

# Introduction to Cemetery Hill

Mollie Sanders passed away in March of 1957. It was an event that tore through my mind and left almost a cosmic devastation. Her passing was so crushing that I was determined to push blindly forth in a path of books and poetry, not worrying anything at all about past, present, or future—a path which led quickly to Thomas, Eliot, Ginsberg, Pound, Sappho, Homer, and Hesiod.

A year later I went to New York City to study at New York University, and began to attend Beat Generation poetry readings in Greenwich Village near the university. I also commenced my studies in ancient Egyptian civilization, and I began to have this sense of my mother floating upon the sky at the moment of her death in an Egyptian boat, high over Lake Tapawingo against the brilliance of a star-lit sky, and above the limestone outcroppings at the top of Cemetery Hill.

In 1959, I read Allen Ginsberg's great poem "Kaddish" in a literary magazine, and then that fall wrote a sequence of poems called "Threinos—Dirge for Mollie Sanders." My girlfriend, and future wife, Miriam Kittell, read "Threinos" and encouraged me to become a poet, an encouragement which, coupled with that of my high school English teacher, Lecie Hall, was all that I needed to begin my profession.

Toward the end of 1961, I was reading John Cage's *Silence* one evening, and was struck by the way he had created pages with multiple columns of short-lined verse. I was thinking of that Egyptian death barque floating above the lake with my mother aboard. That very night I began the sequence of poems called "Cemetery Hill."

Throughout the 1960s and decades beyond, I added poems about Mollie to this memorial.

Mollie sitting on a Running Board

Mollie around age 18 or 19

# Cemetery Hill

The Scene: March 7, 1957—Cemetery Hill—at the foot of which we lived—11 p.m. death of mother—mother appears in my room, calls name, touches, then floats out to Death Barge—late night vision of the Death Barge floating through the sky & entering the dawn sun-disc.

And the hands
with white veins
There
dropped on me
from above
and
boiling boiling boiling
the breath of fire
came boiling
and the white eyes
floated out upon
the darkness
in my room
& the voice
called out from There
my name:
11 p.m.  March 7
1957: silence,
and floating up over
the hill
beyond the Cemetery
was Apparition
with veins full
of white blood
& white eyes
beaming
berserkness,
Nameless,

a Phantom,
never to enter again
the house she curst
,
& to have grown thin
in the curse house
down from the
Cemetery Hill
where I knew
Death would
enter early
after my
Grandmother
had
misinformed
me about
Death:
"You shall
nevah die."
& my mother
hipping me later
'bout Death
& I ran
out onto the terrace
and faced the Cemetery
up on the hill
where the winter
sun-rise glistened
off the name-plates

There,
Death-Rays
focused into
young-eye;
yes I ran
out on to Terrace
in a death-vulsion,
for Grandmother
had said that
Drs. would
make me live
forever,
& I cried there,
stomped into the
Death-chain,
which I had
fled, age 5,
fled fled;
& always
the sun-shafts
glittering off of
tombstones
on the hill
above
my home
meant Death;
Death was
a hill with
tombstones for
teeth,
a Grandmother,
a mother
without hope,
and in the
mornings
a rain-crow
exuding Death
in the trees;
And day now

puking itself
up over the
Horizon
reflects
on Cemetery
Hill,
beams upon
the ground
where my mother
lies in a beige suit
in a dark brown
coffin,
Ears laden
with earrings,
& a necklace
on the neck;
and on the
night she died
I saw the
Barge of Death
float out into the Black
& the death-ship
full of cakes & vases
entered the Plexus,
freaked itself
in the sun's-eye;
& I heard her voice
at 11 p.m.
silence: March 7, 1957
and she floated
up over the Hill
beyond the Cemetery
& entered the
Sun-barge
& when
dawn
was balling
the Hill
she was

sucked into
the Sun.
.

.
O I have
seen  seen  seen!
her floating
in the Barge
& she was
as a sunflower
invaded by floodlights,
& her eyes
were white
& her veins
were full
of white blood
and her
mind opened out
& the brain-valves
were turned open
and she entered
the Brilliance,
& her mind
was staggered
in the flood
of phenomena;
and I have heard
o I have heard
my mother
on the barge
of death,
seduced into the rainbow,
led into the current,
and Eye flinging freak-beams
on itself,
a telephone book smeared
with blood;
and I have heard my mother
as her shade stomped out

of the steaming flesh,
and her voice claws
out of the night there,
whose hands were
so beautiful,
whose hands
hooked out at the
oxygen tent
as she lay dying,
puked into the death-rattle
bones arattle,
katakakic stompout
of the Blossom!
Frenzy of the
Time-Murrain!
Death-Meat cooling off!
Sunflower    out of the flesh!
All out    all out!
.

.

And then she
went out upon
the Trembling Flank
and went forth upon
the Great Necklace of Energy
& rode out
in the
Death Barge
and entered where
the Scarab
dangled from the Neckstrands
,
and the brain
talked freely,
& she then stood
in a perpetual
tremble
on the Black Back
of the Scarab

and she was caught up
in the whirr of wings
There,
& she became full
in the great
Plasm of Being,
& her Eye-Heart-Mind
went berserk in the
desire and fulfillment.
.
.

Eyebrow
in the time-blossom
Ear swiveled in
to th' Nipple,
drool drr
ripping
in the Cascade,
brow into
Breast-Gulf
& her mind
entered
the Vastness
& the Cosmos
quaked,
& her Eye
entered upon
itself
in deliverance,
&
forever into
tremble and nothing,
always into
tremble and nothing,
Last Breath
into
tremble and nothing,
Spiritus Aeterna
into

tremble and nothing,
Crotch entering
into the
Word-machine,
Eyelash
dragged over
the time-stream,
ejaculata
in cosmo,
the Dark
enters
& reenters
the flesh
and the
Vagina
comes into being
around the
endless Phallus,
& the heart
appears
beyond the Eye
& forever
verberates
in the time-plex,
and
she enters
in continuing
desire
with the
Angeloi,
tense & bristling
on the terrace
of stars;
and "word-lines"
were crushed
in the
Vibrata
& were
to the ear

as resin
in a
foot fetish,
and Hello
out there!
cry of the
Shade
& she was
caught up
in the
utter Roar,

Plexus now,
no more
in the Vortex
but
became
the Vortex,
became the
Lamb &
the blood
flowing
out of Lamb

—November 5, 1961
after an evening reading
John Cage's *Silence*

## Arise Garland Flame

Arise! out of me garland flame!
Arise Arise rose wraith
out of my billion back-brain cells
I come I wandering
down to your biered womanness
in your green untombstoned grave
up over the hill
I shall write 4 poems to you
from 4 directions
from the West up Cemetery Hill
from the East along the ridge
from the South up the long slope
from the North along the row of trees and
over the fences

Arise wraith in me
that is of thee
come forth gentle spirit from out my heart
through the power of these
my imperatives.
Enter my brain with flares searing the meat
light up the animal halls
lain dark through these
phylogenous aeons
I shall be your mystes
to paint my flesh &
char my embers in the service
of your gleaming fane
o woman of the Disc
come forth come forth come forth
screaming genius! come forth
I am the meat-chain
born of your legs spread
over the linen
falling in a proskynetical glory
to kiss thy toes dangling

out of a slatted boat
in the dawn:
Blaze up in me hierogyne
that I may examine myself
whom you made whom you
rolled from your legs
in the service of Replication
Blaze up with your eyes painted
the myriad arms of the DISC to
lift you finally
up from the showered halo
dawn sun over the protestant stones
Death Boat stroked by the Arms
fingers slid along brow
to touch the Eye
blinked
open in the Boat
mouth free to pucker or smile
hands heating the forehead long lain electricity still

all all all hands all moving
all from the sun-disc all from the boat
all in the radial fingers
all from your rising, Mollie,
burn, rise in me your son,

come forth!
wet woman bathing
breast poked with
a lonely finger
shoulder & back
washed by the
tiny hands
to know her

bush fragrant
with soap
breasts dangling
over the hairy heads
You, Robert, & I
wet children
from your crotch
under the faucet,
The memory gleams!
plates of armor
fall from the psyche
the water scalds
with our love

We are one
line of replication,
the meat-chain
spurts from the legs,
We are the
first slimy thing that
bubbled out of a warm
water spring
in the kryptozoic aeon,
the line of
evolution hangs
from the prostate,

Arise wet woman Mollie mother
bathed & beautiful
free from the strangle of
the slick, scented satin rubbed
over your face & the
ruffles pressed down on your nostrils.
Bloom, flare, blink open
or come at least to
my mind, o memory,
where the flares are set
to light up
at your footfall

—June–August 1964

# The Pilgrimage

There is nothing on the
wet morning grass
not even a mound
to mark the grave.
I have started in the
shade of the walnut
trees & walked
up the hill
to make my
proskynesis at thy altar
o daughter of Ra
How elaborately the morning kisses
this hill with its teeth
I faint under the
magic rays of the sun
which devour the ground.
Just to the south
by the wilted flowers
of a grave newly sodded
the rain has forced
a hole that goes
deep down down down to the only Acheron
first finger then stick
I poke to find its end
THERE IS NO END
no tears Ed
worship her with
the flowers you brought
build her a monument of flowers
prothesis of words
in the only adoratio possible.
When I wake I find
the flowers fallen
in the shape
of an arm & hand!
a flower-glyph on the grave lawn!

The hand lies westward
& the arm of flowers points
from the East
where Barque of the Morn
floats forth
with bundles of sun-arms
for Ra's benefaction
with benevolent arms of light
hands out of the disc
peace fingers groping
all the transeminentia
—gathered together—
swathed in Ra

The Arms Arms of Ra
dipping in benemagnificence
hook-hands cusping in gentleness
smooth arms from the disc
over the cemetery
the raincrow at peace now
storm over, wet dew, hot sun
only the wet grave newly sodded
drawing my Eye down
to Acheron Acheron of All
at the end of the rain tube
under the brown bronze lid
& above the satin
Acheron Acheron Acheron

—July 1964

## For Mollie Sanders

*1903–1957*


It has been hard
living without you
dear mother

when the cold fog
rolls at our feet
from Lake Tapawingo

or when your memory
floods our brain

Love forever,

your husband, your sons, your daughter


—Early 1967
thinking to have it printed
in March in the
*Jackson County Democrat*

# Visit to the Sodden Grass

*—A dream is from Zeus*
—Homer

*After my book on the Manson group was published in late '71 I*
*visited Kansas City to see my brother and father, plus old friends.*
*My father, Lyle, and I drove out to Cemetery Hill to see Mollie's*
*stone, which not long before had been laid in place.*

> With Lyle
> bought a red & white
> carnation spray
> from Luther's
> flower shop
>
> tears in the florist's

& then the drive
to Cemetery Hill

KCMO

> Dolly Parton
> "Back to the seasons of my youth"
>
> "How my mama put the rags to use!"
>
> Black guy
> on 63rd
> standing
> bells w/ roses on them
>
> & a lady in car at stoplight
> X8PI35 maroon Mercury
> w/ rotted confederate flag
> on the left rear window
>
> teased hair mesomorph
> whacked down the window door lock

after grabbing a visual

•

Past KC Chiefs practice field
past the northern end
                of Swope Park
where we had our senior picnic
                there under the sacred
                                blanket of touch

•

            & the little drive-in restaurant
            at 40 & Noland
                    where Bud Kern tried to
                    beat me up

            is now a House of Pancakes

Dusey's Truckstop is gone!
where we went to dance after basketball games in '56

(No One Under 18 Admitted:
the x-rated H-way 40 drive-in!
What would Judy's mother
        have said in 1956 coming back
                        from an x-rated flick?)

Snell's Mobile Hotel
        court
            is still there

Hello Phyllis Snell
Remember the
prom of '56?

            White Oak School
                still
                there

Roger Devodere's

house
banked by lakes

(the quarterback on my 8th grade team)

with an old miniature golf course
grown up with weeds
        near where we used to swim

& a new mobile home park
has rape-scoured ten feet of the topsoil down

           •

On the right!
Crackerneck Country Club
        new since I been gone

And then past Valley View Road!
the home of what they used to call the
Devil's Backbone
        where we parked after the prom  o' '57

           •

And then, the Hill

kissing the
rosy granite

weeping

for the ten carnations
in the rain-sodden dirt

        "Back to the seasons of my youth"

         & then on back to the City
         with my Dad

—December 16, 1971

## Cemetery Hill: A Tune for the Pulse Lyre

Twenty-four years have gone
and I see you still
standing in your black suit & veil
on Cemetery Hill

They say   some day   in the solar wind
giant ships shall sail
There'll be no thinking then     how lovers fail
their fortunes to bind

In the sky above   the foggy lake   the boat set sail
bearing my mother away
to the end of the sky        where they stub out the torch
                            and they empty the boat
on the shores of the Lake of Fire

          They stub out their torches
          in pitchers of milk
          on the shores of the Lake of Fire

          They stub out their torches
          in pitchers of milk
          of the shores of the Lake of Fire

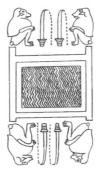

There've been so many many     broken hearts
the sky should be red

but the solar wind    oh it didn't care    & we didn't dare
our fortunes to wed

but twenty-four years have gone
and I see you still
standing in your black suit & veil
on Cemetery Hill


—1981

# Glory of the '60s

# Pindar's Revenge

Ἄριστον μὲν ὕδωρ
*"Water is the greatest thing"*
—Pindar

I know that the sun rising
is a temporary thing,
that the sun obtuse on clouds
at 30 thousand feet from the
airline windows is an
equal particle, that
Ra is a shard, an
ostracon from a forbidden
cycle of the aeons.
Nor god nor pulsing phantom forever
but that I live at the mansion of earth
for 80 years in the warmth,
the children off to space,
the chickens still crowing
at sunup, but our
hearts beat lugubrium   lugubrium   lugubrium
at Ra's pink-fingered sinking

42 billion years
then zap
then 42
zap
we are caught

The meat chain
born of the prostate,
born of the
cusping egg—
caught, ended,
slashed. We are
led by the calf
to the thin

arroyo
to be slaughtered in droves
driven into the eyes and
slashings of the manglers,
that little drama,
no matter,

42
zap
"we are now
in the
electromagnetic
cycle"

IT lives.
Enormous breathings
& compressions
of IT

—July 24, 1965
returning to NY, 30,000
feet, from the Berkeley Poetry
Conference. The quote and
the concept of the 42 billion
year zap, are from Charles Olson's
lectures at the conference.

## The Leaves of Heaven

The leaves of heaven
are ever greene,
& the leaves of the
soul are Sere
and cold

I have failed
my mother
& she has
failed me

Everything about
a human
is doomed
his life, his
things, his
hope, his
work

The pallbearer
barfs on the
diaper

The phantoms,
The phantoms,
what to do
about the
phantoms?

Kiss a hot
wet lightbulb.

—1967

# Whence Came the Etruscans?

*—a prophesy of 1968*

I shall prophecy
the source of Etruria.
Nor from Lemnos
nor from Lydia
but
from
Scandinavia
to there
from a warm
water spring area
since snuffed
in the Ural Mntns.

a
God told me
this scoffing human
scanning these columns,

in a dope-trance
on a sleazy rock & roll tour
in the fall
of 1968.

I believe the numen.

## On the Road in Oregon

May 3rd, '68, the Fugs drove to Eugene, Oregon
just about the very time
the students were occupying the streets of Paris
to play at a club called the Lemon Tree
                              by a beaver pond

Before the performance
I walked out to water's edge
I had to go back in my mind
to the lakes of my youth
to Olson's Belovéd Lake
to find such a sense of peace
or Elvis Presley's rendition of
                    "Peace in the Valley"
                         which helped me through
                              the grief of my mother's death

It was the best time for me in '68
and I jotted it down for the files:

        "*From an Oregon Tour*

                    (a)

        Do not treat us as loathsome dirt
        o God,

        who have not chosen,
        nor kill us too soon
        before we might have
        touched or seen.

        I will brave
        the twistings of wind,

        to meet Thee

above the v-shaped
trail of the beaver
in the stream.

I will hold within
the shriveled core of fear,

that I might find
Thee in the spirits

of the glen
in the first-glazed
ghosts of mist I see adrift awhirl aswirl
upon the dusk-ivory water

in some body-sense of pax
at last
after 28 young years

(b)

the steam rises above the broken branches
the beaver seen from the window of the nightclub
mixed-log harmony
fills us with longing for the unutterable modes
of the marvelous
before we must climb onto the stage and sing
to the buckskin paisley painted patrons.

It will not be for long
that we will be alone
we are the batter
poured and impuissant."


After that jotting
        I left the mixed-log harmony of
                        the beaver dam,
    and sang, drank, smoked pot, & partied
                    till the pink straps of hempsandal dawn
                    did blush above the motel.

# The Entrapment of John Sinclair

## Prologue

By the fall of 1971 I had just gone through two very intense years writing my book on the Manson group, *The Family*. I was upset that my friend the poet and cultural leader John Sinclair had been in prison in Michigan now for over two years, sentenced to ten years for giving a couple of joints from a cookie jar in Detroit to an undercover police officer who'd been posing as a hippie. I decided to raise my voice in protest.

While researching my book, I had been on the staff of the excellent alternative paper, *The Los Angeles Free Press,* writing articles about the Manson family murder trial, which I attended for a number of months. In the early fall, as *The Family* was being published, I wrote the long poem, "The Entrapment of John Sinclair," which the *Free Press* printed in its entirety.

Meanwhile, that same set of weeks John Lennon and his wife Yoko Ono had decided to move to New York City. John Lennon's great song "Imagine" had been released in early November.

One afternoon John and Yoko visited John Cage on Bank Street in Greenwich Village. The drummer Joe Butler lived next door, and somehow John and Yoko learned that Butler's storefront apartment was for rent. The couple decided to take the place and soon they moved in.

Miriam, I, and our daughter Deirdre were living in the Village about three blocks from Lennon and Ono's newly rented apartment. I was feeling a bit burned out after a full two years investigating a creepy group of murderers and their cult. Shortly after Lennon moved into Bank Street, I began to have problems with my home phone. Often when I tried to make a call, I heard a male voice with an English accent on the line. I was investigating a creepy English cult at the time, so to hear a English voice on my line was not pleasant. The matter was soon cleared up. The telephone company claimed that our lines were accidently crossed with John and Yoko's, and so we soon each had our own separate numbers.

It was around that time that Lennon read "The Entrapment of John Sinclair" in the *Free Press* and became interested in the case. I went to a meeting with Lennon and Ono at their new apartment, where among the things discussed was doing a series of concerts across America to help Sinclair get his release from jail; also possible activities for peace at the Republican National Convention, then scheduled for San Diego in the summer of 1972.

Plans began for a major concert to demand Sinclair's release. On December 10, at a packed Crisler Arena in Ann Arbor that sold out in four hours, John Lennon sang a new tune, "It Ain't Fair, John Sinclair." Also on the bill were Stevie Wonder (with a wondrous version of "Superstition,") Bobby Seale, Allen Ginsberg, Phil Ochs, Archie Shepp, and others. I read a section from "The Entrapment of John Sinclair."

John was released just a few days later. Meanwhile the infamous Division 5 of the FBI sent out a memo calling for 24/7 surveillance of the new Lennon/Ono apartment on Bank Street:

"It has come to the . . . attention of this office that John Lennon, formerly of the Beatles, and Yoko Ono Lennon, wife of John Lennon, have intentions of remaining in this country & seeking permanent residence therein . . . this has been judged to be inadvisable and it is recommended that all applications are to be denied. Their relationships with one (6521) Jerry Rubin, and one John Sinclair (4536), also their many commitments which are judged to be highly political and unfavorable to the present administration . . . Because of this and their controversial behavior, they are to be judged as both undesirable and dangerous aliens . . . Your office is to maintain a constant surveillance of their residence . . ."

The government began a big project to toss Lennon from the United States. They bugged him, and I heard they also rented an apartment across from their Bank Street place, to keep tabs on them. John Lennon may have been a hero to 100s of millions, but the henchmen of Richard Nixon hungered to force him to undergo a political perp-walk.

For the next few years the Nixonites did their best to deport him, but, with the help of his many fans, and good lawyers, Lennon prevailed, and now his "Imagine" is played as an international anthem just before midnight for the millions watching the New Year's ball drop on Time's Square.

And John Sinclair still thrives.

## The Entrapment of John Sinclair

If justice ever
comes to Michigan
the people will
tremble with rage
when they hear
the tale

how a hunk of
lunatic vomit-gunge
named Lieutenant Warner Stringfellow

of the Detroit
police    narcotics    department
undertook    a scheme    lasting several months
                                in late 1966
in order    to entrap    John Sinclair for
                                smoking the peace.

In this entrapment
John gave
a bearded undercover cop
and his simulated wife, also a
undercover cop,
two thin joints
after they had begged
John for weeks
please John
please give us
some grass
please
John
please

John got 10
years for these
two joints
rolled as a gift.

For
three long years
Stringfellow

harassed, harangued,
& hated

set John up
for three arrests

in a hideous neuralgea
of events

       all for his poetry
       all for hiero-hemp
       all for his leadership
       all for his friendships
              into the face of racist
              lieutenants twisted into
              hate-mush

It began in '64
John had graduated
from the University of Michigan
with a B.A. in English
class of 1964.

In the early fall
same year
enrolled in grad school
Wayne State U, Detroit
where he was writing a masters

thesis on
William Burroughs

On October 6, 1964
he was arrested for
"sale and possession of marijuana"

In those
days of October 1964 there was a laughable
State Law in fair-shored Michigan
that dealt out life imprisonment
for sale and possession of the
yellow-flowered herb.

Accordingly,
John pled guilty to a reduced charge
and was put on probation
for two circles of the sun.

        While this hassle
        was shrieking,

    John and friends were getting together
    in the frontiers of modern music and
    poetry.

    On November 1, 1964 John and 16 fellow
    musicians and poets
    formed the
    Artists' Workshop
    in the city of Detroit.

It's simply not possible
to list the
        100s of poetry readings
        100s of concerts
          of tracts
            & books
              & leaflets

    produced by the Artists' Workshop
    in '64 & '65 & '66

They soared aloft
to Charles Olson's
              *Projective Verse*

and Don Allen's anthology
*The New American Poetry*

     and the music of Sun Ra and
     Coltrane and Archie Shepp and
     Pharaoh Sanders and Marion Brown
     and . . .

Picked up
that word
abandoned
     in the chamber of commerce: freedom
     filled their lungs
     with freedom

wrote freedom

     played freedom music

fucked in freedom
when guilt corroded the eyeballs
staring in the supermarket

     Stringfellow
     hated the friendship
     black and white together we shall not
     be moved
        Artists' Workshop
     Hated the confident humans
     puffing on
        prairie peace fires
        above the round
        yellow screens

     He hated the
     free concerts

     Hated the
     Thursday night
     poetry classes

Hated love?

Hated the
share-all-things
share pot
          of leaf
          pot of food.

John wrote this
in 1964
               to tell of their intention
               to put down radical roots
               in a Michigan city


". . . a conscious community of artists and lovers who
live together, work together, share all things—
smoke dope together, dance and fuck together, and
spread the word together everyway we can—through
our dress, our freedom of movement, our music
and dance, our economy, our human social forms,
through our every breath on this planet."

               Leni & John got married
               in June of 1965

               In July John read
               at the Berkeley Poetry Conference
               at the U of California

               He was the music editor of
               the *Fifth Estate*   newspaper   Detroit

               He wrote two books of poems in '65
               The Workshop grew

and Stringfellow kept
up the pressure

On August 16, 1965

after a so-called "three week investigation"
directed by Lieutenant Stringfellow
25 policemen waited outside
for a signal from a brave undercover agent

that he had been able to make a buy
of an herb used medicinally
by George Washington and
    Thomas Jefferson

                        After this second arrest
                        Lieutenant Stringfellow
                        was all over
                        the papers
                        issuing quotes against
                        John's influence
                        among John's fellow young.

        On
    2/24/66
        a judge
        at the Recorders Court
        gave him
        6 months
                at the
                Detroit House of Corrections
                a.k.a. DeHoCo

        even though prominent people
        rallied to his support with
        letters and pressure.

    On August 5, 1966
    John was released from the
Detroit House of Correction
& right away
resumed his frenzied activities
for poetry, socialism, pax-herb
& song-dance
not to mention
sun-dance.

Within
12 days
of his release
he had printed
several magazines
& a book of
his poems called
FIRE MUSIC
& he was off
to NY
for a visit.

Enter Stringfellow.

In late Aug
or early Sept
            1966
a 41 year old    narcotics
under    cover    officer    named
Vahan Kapagian began to grow a beard
upon the orders of Lt. Warner Stringfellow

in order to try to entrap
distributors and users
of the far-famed Leaf

On October 5, 1966
Lieutenant String-penis, or whatever
his name is,
was sneaking around at night in the buildings
housing the Artists' Workshop
on John Lodge, a street in Detroit.

Stumbled
            into
                        John Sinclair's apartment

He hadn't seen John for a year.
Was two years to the day
since the String had first
arrested him

His language was schizophrenic.
The newt-nark chuckled asking John:

> "When are you gonna write
> a story on me, John?"

> ha  ha

And later spewing hate upon his
poet victim:

> "I know what you are—
> and when I get you again I'll
> drown you, you worthless prick."

Right away
    John wrote

POEM FOR WARNER STRINGFELLOW

> which was
> published as a book
> by the Artists' Workshop Press
> 2 days after Warner'd
> honked into John's apartment

On October 7–8, 1966 John and Leni and
lover-friends began to give their time and co-
operation to the rock and roll and dance
events at the Grande Ballroom,

> in Detroit. There they could
> speak to people by the thousands
> which must have agnewed-off the
> good Lieutenant.

They sold their publications there.
They ran the light show.
They held benefits.
Began to inspire local rock bands.
In a plan to try to send out
a few harmonic quiverings
from the Iron Flower.

By the middle
of October 1966
the undercover cop Kapagian     a.k.a.
                Louie

had grown a sufficient beard
& hair to look for
trusting marks.

He was hired to work
at the Candle Shop
                on Plum Street,
an area of Detroit—in common
with most American cities—where
there were established those incense,
candle, dope-pipe, poster and record
shops replete with psychedelic gew-gaws.

Temporary zones of revolt and freedom.

Then
freshly-bearded Louie the Candle Shop nark-punk
was assigned by Lieutenant Stringfellow
to attend on October 18, 1966

                a poetry reading!!!
                given by John Sinclair
                at Lower LeRoy Auditorium
                on the campus of
                Wayne State University.

In his testimony at Sinclair's trial,
Louie the Nark dredged from his ill-witted
mind that the meeting was "mixed"—as
he termed it, containing both "Negro and
white" listeners—

                which must have shocked the
                heroin-white Lieutenant.

On October 28, 1966
Louie the Candle Nark went
to the Grande Ballroom
  "to become part of the group of
  youngsters who were attending these
  dances"—as he testified.

Enter a woman nark.

 Jane Mumford Lovelace, a.k.a. Pat Green—her under
 cover cop name—had been a Detroit Police Dept
 officer for three years.  At the end of November
 1966 she was assigned to the narcotics division
 and was given the heroic task of infiltrator-informer.
 Jane Mumford Lovelace a.k.a. Pat Green posed as
 Vahan Kapagian (a.k.a. Louie the Candle Creep)'s wife,

    and together
    they strove
    to lure John
    Sinclair to sell.

  Lo! around November 30, 1966
  there was an ad in an issue
  of the newspaper *Fifth Estate*
  for a LEMAR meeting the following week

  to be held at the Artists' Workshop
  plexus of community buildings
  Hot Dope!—they thought.
  we can find us some set-ups
  so on December 6
  Louie and Pat

    gamboled in tandem
    to a meeting called by
    John Sinclair himself to

begin a Committee to Legalize Marijuana
8 or 10 people sitting discussing planning

around a table
at 4863 John Lodge.

Kapagian wanted to see if
Sinclair would recognize him
since Kapagian had had a hand
in arresting him
in the past.

But Louie passed
the weirdness test
& he and his wife
were accepted

Sell us some grass John.

The Artists' Workshop
became
Trans-Love Energies
in late '66

Sell us some grass John.

Kapagian and Lovelace infiltrated LEMAR
assisted w/ typing
putting together booklets
sweeping up the place

They
saw Sinclair maybe
6 times

as time oozed.

They even attended Trans-Love communal dinners
on Sundays
One time they even brought along
some fried chicken.

Sell us some grass John.

On December 20, 1966
Kapagian
   was helping
   to type
   at Trans-Love

"The person (not John) who seemed to be in charge"—
   according to Louie's testimony
   requested that Louie come back
   on the 22nd
   to type some more
   on grass tracts

  & Louie the Nark learned that day
  that John was residing in an apartment
  up above the LEMAR meeting place.
  Halleluyah!

Sell us some grass John.

   On Dec 21
   Kapagian again visited the Trans-Love
   buildings
     & mentioned that he
     was going to go somewhere
     in order to cop hemp.

   The Day of the famous
   gesture of friendship
   that got John 10 for 2
   was 12/22/66

   Lieutenant Stringfellow
   and the two undercover hippie cops
   along with another officer named Taylor
   in the late afternoon
   drove directly
   in unmarked police vehicles

   from police headquarters

Narcotics Bureau
to Trans-Love Energies
at 4863 John Lodge

where Stringfellow secreted himself
in an alley
4 houses west of the
Artists' Workshop
& Taylor was stationed in another cop car
across the Freeway
facing the
storefronts.

Pat the Nark
remembered at the trial
that on 12-22-66
she wore
black leotards          black mini skirt
blue sweater            black & gold blouse

All Patrolman Louie
could remember
was that he
was clothed

The two undercover hippies
were wired to
Lt. Stringfellow's unmarked car
in the alley
by means of a Port-A-Talk Unit
stashed in their fake hippie threads

Thus the Lieutenant
could cop some thrill-gasms
listening to the set-up.

Off marched Louie & Pat.
Their purpose:

Sell us some grass John.

They entered
Trans-Love to type
at 5:40 p.m.

John arrived around 7 p.m.
He said hello

John asked Kap
if he had gotten taken care
of

And the narcos said

Give us some grass john.

At 7:20 p.m.
John picked up his saxophone
& went to the storefront
next door to
practice with the band

& shortly thereafter
Kapagian told Mumford
to go next door
to flirt for dope

She interrupted
John who
said that later maybe
he could fix her up
then resumed the tune
& Jane went back
to the other office
to help the other cop
to type for LEMAR

An hour and 1/2 later
the hippie cops told
John they had to leave.

Give us some grass John.
Somewhat reluctantly
he took them upstairs
into his house

where Jane and Louie
sat on a cot in the
kitchen feigning
hemp-hunger.

John reached up

on the shelf
& grabbed down
a brown porcelain
sugar bowl
full of Gentle.

Sinclair rolled a j
handed it to Kapagian
who handed it to Mumford
who put it
in a Kool Cig Pack

Sinclair rolled another
offering to smoke
but Kapagian
in an example of his
slovenly, crude manners
refused—some jive
about it making him dizzy
driving

Then the two cops
with their Port-A-Talk unit

& alley-way monitor
told John they had to
split to the West Side
& this they did
at 9:10 p.m.
for a rendez-vous
with Warner Stringfellow

The narkoids
inked their initials
on the joints
& placed them within a
signed, dated envelope.

These flakes of Ra
were sent to
the lab
where identity
was made
by looking under the micro-
          scope

for small
peculiar hairs that exist
on grass-leaves and
by a chemical pot test
revealing
11.50 grains of cannabis
                    sativa

              Give us some
                    grass
                    John

What a triumph
for law and order

but they still hadn't
been able to buy any

so Louie kept calling
the Trans-Love office
"to maintain the contact"—as
                    he later testified.
On December 27, 1966
Kapagian
helped carry stuff

upstairs into
the new quarters
on John Lodge

still trying to buy.

        On Dec 28
        the cop tried again
        to buy mj
        from John
        but John
        threw that
        old donut into
        the air

On Jan 24, 1967
John was arrested
w/ 55 other people
in a
        "campus" grass raid—
        33 days after
        John oped the brown crock
        to give.

John brushed aside
the snarls
        of nark-hate

fell back into his usual
pale blurr of total frenzy

after he was bailed out
and the months passed

He wrote a book
*Meditations: a Suite for John Coltrane*
in February 1967

Their beautiful daughter
Marion Sunny Sinclair
was born in May 4th

In August '67
John began to manage
the rock band MC5

His friends
tended to forget
about the pot charge
over his head

That was the way he
wanted it—why worry.

                    Trans-Love moved
                    with the assembled families
                    to Ann Arbor in June of 1968

John and the MC5
were the only rock band
to show
in Lincoln Park
to play during the
Democratic National Convention
in August '68.

                    Co-
                    founded the
                    White Panther Party
                    in Nov
                    '68

serving as Minister of Information.

Most of the cases
involving those arrested in the
same campus raid back in '67
were thrown out of court.

When John
was finally tried

during the week of
the moon walk
1969 July

The charge was possession
and the penalty
was a possible
<u>one</u> to 10 years
in jail

On July 25          the jury found him
guilty of           possession!
                    of the mandible's quantity
                    of hemp

                    then Judge Columbo
                    the fascist churl
                    held him over in
                    jail without bail
                    pending sentencing on
                    July 28, 1969

                    2 1/2 years
                    after his arrest

& in an atmosphere
of hostile publicity
given to him by
the local newspapers.

It was a fascist's Monday
July 28, 1969

when the trial judge
Robert J. Columbo
a name to remember

sentenced John to
jail with these words:

"John Sinclair has been out to show that the law means
nothing to him and to his ilk. And that they can violate
the law with impunity and the law can't do anything
about it. Well, the time has come. The day has come.
And you may laugh, Mr. Sinclair, but you will have a
long time to laugh about it. Because it is the judgement
of this court that you, John Sinclair, stand committed
to the state prison at Jackson or such other institution as
the Michigan Corrections Commission may designate . . ."

remember his name
remember his name

"for a minimum term of not less than nine and a half nor
more than ten years. The court makes no recommendation
upon the sentence other than the fact that you will be
credited for the two days you spent in the county jail."

Then the judge denied bond which
would have set him free
pending appeal

& John was gone
from the set.

**SET HIM FREE!**

Putting someone
under surveillance
is easy enough

if you want
to play the
game of nark-hate

& many hours
of glum contemplation
I've spent

thinking of putting
Warner Stringfellow
& Judge Robt Columbo
under surveillance

to see what they
really do
with their time

buy a few black market
xeroxes of their
bank accounts

run a credit check
and property check
and a greed check

because there's
something laughable
& sadistic going on

especially when
heroin is sold like candy
in Detroit

& drug wars
leave people shot dead
all over town

while the chief of under
cover assignments
Lt. Warner Stringfellow
chases down a poet.

If John Sinclair
were a thug
selling heroin to grade school children
& paying bribes to police and public officials

        he'd be a free man today

If John Sinclair
were a pilot for Air America
dumping polyethylene bags of opium/heroin
in the Gulf of Siam

        he'd be a free man today

If John Sinclair
were shaking down bar owners
in Pontiac
forcing mafia juke boxes down scared throats

        he'd be a free man today

If John Sinclair
had bayonetted Vietnamese women
or smashed off their face-skin with
bamboo mallets

        he'd be a free man today

      Two years after
      his sentenc-
      ing

      it curses our miserable death-trampled
      lives
      that John should still be
      enslaved in the mind of
      Stringfellow/Columbo

And that's what it is
where John lies buried
in boulders & steel

o subtle currents of power
o rainbow humans roaming like Blake-folk
set him free
set a gentle
man free.

The only answer
is pressure

and a solemn declaration
before the
boundless universe:

Love & public          & a huge screaming mob
tranquility                  outside the homes
& sharers' bliss       of every official
for those who              who keeps
help him free          John Sinclair in jail.

—August-Sept-Oct
1971

# Dreams of Sexual Perfection

*Nam castum esse decet pium poetam*
*ipsum, versiculos nihil necesse est*

—*Catullus 16*

## Sheep-Fuck Poem

The ba ba lanolin fur-ears

        sex
     Trembling Lamb
where I enter the
        matted meat
of the trembly sheep
the cunt warm
    & woman sized
offered by the lamb
which is surely the
lamb of god, the
lamb of the Trembling Flank
& the bucking & sighing
when the prick sputs
the hot come
      into loins
& the lamb looks back
with her eye
   & glazes me
in the freak-beams
& we are oily & atremble
  in the lanolin glaze
     frenzy morning field
    hay hidden
       fuck-lamb
   day in bloom torrent.

—November '61,
February '62

## Elm-Fuck Poem

in to the oily crotch
place dick

go up
kiss the grey-white tree
fondle the crotch
sweet juice there flowing

to which you place the tongue
to suck the pulse of the

Hamadryad

come into the cool grey
bark  the hair-grey color of Persephone

how difficult it is
to be fucked
in the volcano!

ahhhhh but how sweet
the elm tree's rheuming
grey bark made black
by the viscid
fluid flowing

out of the branches—

I place my dick
in the tight in-folds of the elm v
—heat of the summer—

fuck till the come drift
down thru the bark-furrows
fuck thru the warm afternoon

sperm steams in the sun

birds in the branches
sun shines thru
seed steam
thru
wing of butterfly
wetting its
furry fluttering tips


I have given myself to the elm
I have soaked the dryad's shawl
What a wonderful world,
a palace of gentle sexual aggression.

Tree baby!
how I love to rim
your bark slits
kiss the leaves
above your dripping
elm crotch oozing
at the base

I place my penis
over the mish

& slowly start to
shove it deeper
encasing it into deep deep elm snatch

Let me sing
of a need to fuck
at once the tousled leaf elm
place the lingam
in wet tree oil—
slowly o lovely lady,
such care & kindness
—as when rabbit nose
snoozles a carrot—

> but give it thrill jabs,
> give it to her,

worship the Dryad
fill her with foaming

under the elm boughs
heavy in the summer wind

to fill all holes,
lovely longing lone lingam
plugging the vastness.

Do you feel it, pretty humans,
& do you know

a tree-twat is as good as
a buttock
& the elm branch is the dryad's breast

—1966

## Holy Was Demeter Walking th' Corn Furrow

It was impossible for one to read
C. Kerényi's *Eleusis* and *Eleusis and the
Eleusinian Mysteries* by George Mylonas,
without falling in love with Demeter.
In 1967, this love was combined with a
long-visioned *idea* of making love w/ the Earth!
That is, the visionary embodiment of
the Egyptian sem-ta ⚱ i.e., earth-fuck. Such a

possibility, as felt in early '67, triggered
off a hunger for instant Elysium. The vision
was of a plowed field—springtime—bright
sunlight—and Demeter, her arms full-laden
with corn sheaves, approaches the angst-eyed
earthling, Edward Sanders, in April 1967,
as a personal *Be-In* that raised the earthling's
mind for all his life to the Permanent Nodule.

The first version of his poem was prepared for
a reading w/ Ted Berrigan at Israel Young's
Folklore Center on Sept. 5, 1967.

---

Fucked the corn-meat
sprouted of the river
in the festish of the lob.

Sucked off the corn-clits
curly and cute
in the earth squack

spurt strands swirling
the soil

When Deo walked down
the dusty spring road
I nearly fell afaint

I tried to
tell her "I am
no Poseidon"

but she smiled
& said this: "O earthling
even a poet
as thou art,
and a punkly one,
can be a thrill
to the λουσία

for I have been
washed in the River!
And all are good!
And oh how I shall love
thee,
little pale poet of earth!"

Not a word more mouthing,
Demeter,
pale as husk fibres,
shy as new corn
        near to the
                husk tip

bent over the furrow
with blessings,
by the fresh-plowed river bank

Total Beauty in the odors
of new sprouted dirt.

Bent over     Bent down
& I flipped it to the
buns, and knew the
god-rose in the snatch

felt the god-butt
knew her &
spurted thru the
blessings, droplets
of spangled jissom
in the Red Halls of
Demeter, the Goddess.
Pumped in the berry bushes
to know her, suck off
the wineberries
smeared on her buttocks
ate Demeter, corngirl,
out of her salinity
ahhh   &8   ahhh   &8   ahhh

            Demeter    pale as husk-fibres
            shy as new corn
                  near to the
                        husk tip

            Total Beauty in the odors
            of new sprouted dirt.

            A mocha milk shake
            is not so sweet
            as your buns
            pouring out
                  the godly
                      bun gush

        And then Demeter
        turned around
        and sank to her
        knees   knee caps sink
        out of sight
        in the plow-clods,
        white goddess-palms
        reach up
        rub my knees
        & then to suck
        my poor pale
        earthling prong—

see her crouched there
(the vision, forever in mind, of)
husk fibers hanging out of ass
white new corn
is as white as her
lip-padded chomp teeth
O-ing my pole.

      And later
      a flash spread
      in loam dirt

      leg of the Deo to th' south east
      leg of the Deo crookt up
              to th' south southwest

      the back of her snug
      in a sure 'n' perfect
      north-south furrow

      I shall kiss the fibres
      shall buss th'
      o'er laid soil with
      wan lips & desirable

      freckles of your
      belly as Indian
      corn in an
      autumn bundle.

    Torrid was th' goddess groin
    tongue-moth frying
    in the
    candle of the earth-clit

And maybe you think
that when dark Deo came
that it was not
a different experience—

      One wd have thought
      that the gods were rerunning
      the submergence of Atlantis

                    so much did
                  the plow-plot
                quake around us
                      as my poet's tongue
              flash-flitted my Deo
                    10,000 times
            till grope-quake
        seized her crotch's
            pink lick-node

              "ahh, sweet
        poet of earth," she cried

        "o sing to me
              sing to me."

    & the pale beams of the
Cosmic Intrusion
                    enter
      the brain—

        glorious Da-Mater
        walking away—

        oh watch her walk away!

        dripping my come over
        cornleaf, back
        to her bower among the deathless,

        burnished buttocks etching the Sky—
        honed of a finer tool than ever
        carved a grope grape—rose
        leaves not as interesting as
        the wrinkles of her ass
        ahh for another pinch
        of skuz from thy
        omphalic glory
        my lady of the corn.

        ahh what a thrill is a god grope.

## By Honor, By Agony

by honor

by agony

by the Cretan horns
    by the altar
        of Breasts

ᴦ↙ ᴦ↙ ᴦ↙ ᴦ↙

by the soaking of the
    Dryad's shawl

      & the cool vagina
      hanging from the Elm.

Eat of the Acorn's navel
& suck the sugar of
the Earthworm's logic

—1967

# Adios Diamond Sutra

# Writing *The Family:*
## The Road to Investigative Poetry

While working on my book on the Manson group, I found myself
writing in verse clusters with line breaks. I jotted hundreds of
pages in this manner,
     a path which a few years later led
         to my manifesto *Investigative Poetry*

Two examples from my 1970 note pages:

### 1.
### Fall 1967

It was
  in Topanga
Canyon that
     the group began
to outgrow the
    Black Bus.
It became necessary
more or less to exist vertically—
     to put down roots
    to camp near a friendly house
      or to set up auxilliary tents,

   in order to
     accommodate
   the hemp horde.

### 2.
### Cielo Drive, August 9, 1969

DeRosa
walked in
observed
window open,
lights turned off
saw Steve Parent

Whisenhunt arrived
they both
went back to Parent
then to garage
& the room above
—found nothing

walked to front
and saw two bodies
on the lawn—

Then DeRosa
guarded the front
gun drawn

while Whisenhunt & Burbridge
crawled into the
          nursery window—

After a while DeRosa
"notified his brother officer" inside
& went in the front door
          avoiding the
                blood
saw bodies, "PIG"

Heard Garretson
(in the nearby cottage)—
yelled to Garretson:
   "Freeze!"

          arrested him
          handcuffed him behind back

          Garretson
          claimed
          he tried to make a call
          just as it was getting
          light  (the lines had been cut)

          He waited up longer, till total daylight

then he went to sleep

Dog barking. "Quiet down!"

"The next thing I knew I woke up
and there was an officer pointing a gun at me."

Another officer
also pointed a rifle at him

The door kicked down
Christopher started barking, bit officer

handcuffed him
          threw down
He kept asking what's the matter, what's the matter?

They said they'd show him
They crossed the yard & Garretson
          saw the bodies
Abigail, he thought, at first, was the maid.

          Saw the other one.

Then saw Steve's car
knew there was a body in it
Not sure it was Parent

The rope around the necks
& over the beams,
the "hood-like" towel on the face,
the bodies everywhere, the over kill—this
          was to
          cause officer
          DeRosa
          to seem to
          think it
          to be ritualistic (whatever
                    that meant)

# A Flower from Robert Kennedy's Grave

*During demonstrations at Nixon's second
inauguration, we watched his limo pass, on
the way to the White House; then I drove
over to Arlington Cemetery.*
      *—January 20, 1973*

After
a winding walk
up past the white stones
of snuff,

past the guardhouse
circling circling
around the Catholic henge
to John Kennedy's bright taper
burning on the ground
in windy cold winter after-speech
afternoon

     then walk down
     to the left-hand

          edge of the hill-
          ock—there in speechless serenity,

               built onto the steepness
               a small
               elegant
               perfectly proportioned
               white cross 'bove
               white flat marble marker

               Robert Francis Kennedy

Nearby a fount jets horizontal
over a slab of stone

water curving down abruptly on the
rock front lip

RFK's words of race heal
writ upon the rock above
the flat-fount.

Across the walkway
by the grave
a long red rose
with a vial of water
slipped upon the stem end
& wrapped with shiny tape
lay singly
& to the left of it a
basket of yellow chrysanthemums

and this: that
only a whining hour past
Richard Nixon
oozed down Pennsylvania Avenue
flashing Vs from a limousine
behind a stutter-footed wary pack of marines
their
bayonets stabbing the January
in a thickery of different directions
like small lance hairs
pricked up on the forehead of a
hallucinated drool fiend
during a bummer

but big enough to stab the
throats of hippie rioters

buddy.

I picked a yellow petal

from thy grave
Mr. Robert Kennedy

& brought it home
from Arlington, where many young mourners
stood crying quietly this inauguration day

Picked a dream
        Mr. Robert Kennedy
brought it home in our hearts
burning like a brand in a fennel stalk

Picked a thought-ray
Robert Kennedy

            brought it back from this
            henge of park-side
            eternity

        buses of protesters parked
        in the lots beneath your hill

            Tears splash
            in the vessels
            of the sun

            Picked yellow
            molecules bunched
            in beauty
            from the beauty fount
            Mr. Robert Kennedy

The peace-ark
glides in the vastness,
though weirdness clings to your death.

But nothing can touch the ark
sails through the trellis of evil
brazen, American, wrought of light-hate

Nothing can touch it
not even pyramidal battlements of gore-spore
nor tricky's pitiless flood
of dungeonoid luciphobian losers.

# Sappho on East Seventh

*a sho-sto-po*
*(short story poem)*

*Poet John Barrett was a graduate student in classics at New York
University. His obsession was Sappho—there were drawings of her
on the walls of his apartment as well as photostats of fragments of
her poems found in papier-mâché coffins in Oxyrhynchus, Egypt.
Barrett's translations of her poems were taped above his desk and
the living room was converted into a workshop for the construc-
tion of a four-string lyre with a sounding box fashioned from the
carapace of a European tortoise. John had collected about a dozen
shells. They were in all the rooms—tortoise shells on milk crate
bookshelves used by his friends as ashtrays. He ate his morning
oatmeal out of a shell. The time was late summer. The place East
7th Street near Avenue A.*

He had an obsession for Sappho
He lived inside her meters
like a trout in running mirth

He was building a four-string lyre
to sing Sappho down
Sappho come down

He copied lyres
from the Parthenon frieze
looking for the perfect shape

There were tortoise shells
    hanging by nails
        on the wall

Another lay on his desk
near scraping tools, a saw,
                a pot of glue,
some whittling knives
                from H.L. Wild  (on E. 11th).

Goat horns
        were hard to get
                on the Lower East Side

so he carved the arms
                from the legs
                        of an armchair
                                found in the street

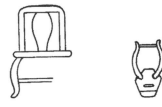

            and a thin rounded sounding board
cut he                (from a spruce wood shingle)
        to fit
                on the shell

The cross bar from arm to arm
        had tuning pegs from
                    an antique broken banjo
                            found in the trash
                                of a burned-out store

A bridge he
        shaped & notched
                from an ebony comb

                and when he had built one
                with which he could sing
                he scribed it with Sappho's

Ἄγε δία χέλυννα μοι
φωνάεσσά τε γίγνεο

"Come my sacred lyre
make yourself sing"

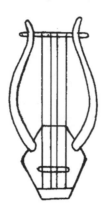

The Lyre
        transformed him—
                in the mode of the
Dada masks
        transforming the shy young poets
                        in the Zurich cabaret.*

Barrett became Some Other Bard
        striding through his rooms
                holding his lyre
        singing with all the passion to summon:

        "There is a river
        in Mitylene

* Referring to the Cabaret Voltaire of 1916 and the spontaneous poem and
dance performance inspired by the donning of Marcel Janco's famous masks.

where Sappho
     used to swim
          with a friend
dropping their sandals
with ivory inlay
     at the water's bank

I saw Sappho
bending in the foam
     peplos-less and chiton free
          on a summer's day

singing a song
     that is lost

They later lay
in the
creekside glade

soothing each other's
skin
     with oil & caresses

singing a song
     that is lost

     O Sappho come down
     Sappho come down."


A friend from school,
     Consuela,
          lived next door
and heard John Barrett's prayer
     through the tenement wall

She listened each night
     to dig what it was
     and finally understood

     when Barrett Sang:

                    "as a glider
                              swoops down
                                        from the cliffs
              over the birchen hills

                    swoop thou down oh
                    Sapph' swoop down"

     She lay in bed
              with her ear
                    to the wall
     spiss-hissing with held back laughs.

     She mocked him:

              "as a cornflake
                              through the
                                        subway grate

              into the
                    bubblegum
                              muck

                    settle thou down
                    Sapph' settle down"

     The next day she told her Greek class
     Together they plotted a trick

     One night   she would
     appear on the fire escape
     she shared with Barrett
     —attired in chiton and peplos*
     and sing/chant some Sappho

---

* The basic attire of ancient Greece, both garments being fashioned from
  oblong pieces of cloth. The chiton was a tunic of linen or wool worn next
  to the skin, doubling around the body. It was pinned over each shoulder,
  and held at the waist by belt or cincture. The peplos was a heavier cloak-
  like overgarment.

as if she were Sappho's haint

She bought a bolt of white linen
on Orchard Street
and brocade for the edges
of Ukrainian symbology
                    at Surma on 7th
                    & sewed herself Sapphic attire

She memorized the "Hymn to Aphrodite,"
Consuela,
                    to sing Sappho down
                    Sappho come down

It was late afternoon when she
came from the shower, donned the chiton
and peplos overgarment,
crawled upon the windowsill, shoved
aside her boxes of flowers


—she knew it was the hour that
                    Barrett would sing—
and crouched upon the gritty
black ironwork
                    blistered and pitted
            from 20 coats in 90 years.

When she heard Barrett's loud
prayer begin and the strings
of his lyre resound, she

stood to sing—Consuela
saw the air above the fire escape
come apart—as if some giant hand
had scissored a line
in reality's tarp

There was a chirping of birds
and dim dots clouding the view.
Through the pointilliste gray
an arm was thrust,
                holding a lyre,
then another arm—
                the fist of it clenched

then opened, and tiny kernels
fell upon the grate
of the fire escape
to rain on the courtyard below

Consuela sank in awe,
the rungs of the fire escape
streaking her knees with grit-gray stripes

while Sappho's body
seemed to float
        through the tarp-warp gap

the very second Barrett's
edge-of-frenzy voice
sang

        "Sappho come down
        come down Sapph'!"

At first John Barrett
            tried to
gaze at the apparition
with an "it's about time" expression

            Then, "Sappho!"  he gasped,
        for actually
            Barrett had little trust
                        in the summoning power

        of a lyre with arms
                    from a scroungéd chair
        and a tremulous voice
                    more like a dare

He glanced about his dis-
hevelled beatnik apartment
and wished he had cleaned away
the bottles from the night before

Sappho picked up his lyre
            from the desk
                    setting her own aside
                            and started to sing

        He could SEE
            the words she sang
        above her
            with a throbbing life of their own

Words of Water

Words of Fire

Words of Broken Oars

When the song was over
　　　　Barrett stood stunned
　　　　　　　　tears on his cheek

sinuses cloggy, vision blurred,
ache of love in his stomach.

Then she walked to the wall
　　　　where he'd pinned
　　　　　　　　his translations

He tried not to glance
　　　　at her breasts
just as he did not look
　　　　in Stanley's Bar
　　　　　　　　on a midriff summer night

The bosom
　　　　of a ghost
　　　　　　　　is not for the kisses
　　　　　　　　　　　　of eyes.

Barrett was horrified
    to see Sappho stand
        reading her verses' versions

It was hard to keep from
        ripping them down.
Finally, she turned away, & laughed,
        "Better than Byron's—
            at least."

Next she visited his shelves
    "Let me gaze upon your
        Book Boat," she said

Oh, no!
    thought John Barrett,
worrying about the many marginal tomes
        in his Book Boat

The gibberish of friends,
    the smut, the
        mal-marked scholarship.

    Sang then Sapph':

"There is a boat
    for every bard
bobbing in the waves
        a Boat of Books

Some will say
            to build a boat of death
Others will sing
            a trimaran of green

But a bard
        had better build
                    a Boat of Books

            for the troublesome
                    flow.

And you shall find
        a Muse for your age
                in the Book Boat prow:

            Retentia
        Muse of the Retained Image.

The pan pipes
        the seven-string lyre
                the arsis & thesis—

        The muses
            with which I sang

were tied
CLIO
EUTERPE
MELPOMENE
URANIA THALIA
POLYHYMNIA
TERPSICHORE
ERATO
to my techniques

but yours is the era
    of captured sunlight
        & oxide-dappled tape

    Retentia
catches the beauteous flow
swifter than a cricket's foot

The photos taped to your wall
of my poem's shreds
      were wrought by
    Retentia

She rushes to the aid of groaning Clio
whose scrolls lie thickened & black

She helps you to sort
      to soothe
        to winnow

    as well as to keep
        to save
          to shape.

The Image is safe
    with Retentia
      for a million years

till the pulsing fires
which scorch all lyres

                    O
Once on an
incurved hillock
            near Mitylene
a circle of maidens sang
                    —Alcaeus was there

            if only
            if only
      I could hear
            their image again!"

Sappho stopped singing
            There was a near-sob tremble
                          in her voice

"Pray to Retentia, John Barrett,
for each muse aids
                    in her measure
and the task
            is to know
the mix of the muses' gifts
                    in your lines."

She moved her hand to the wall
            to touch the photostated papyrus
                    The wall cleaved apart
                          and forth stepped Retentia
                    in a blue-black gown
            crackling on its surface with
                          tiny jiggle-jaggles of lightning
                    which seemed to form
                          almost a lightning lace
                                above the blue-black weave

Barrett was wondering
      what sort of prayer

was proper to utter

in praise of a new muse
        standing in his room
                from the Book Boat prow

He was foolishly thinking
        of scooping the floor
                to kiss Retentia's hem

when Sappho walked to the kitchen cupboard
                        and opened the doors
"What does she want?" Barrett asked himself.
        "I don't have any Methu," he said,
inwardly praising himself for his wit.


(Methu was a famous
        wine produced
                in ancient Lesbos)

"Have you no herb-scented oils?"
                she spoke in complaint,
                shutting the cupboard doors—

    "How frailly you fail
    in matters of love
    & longing," she said

    "How can you think
    a woman like Louise
    would love you,
    knowing what you know?"

She entered Barrett's bedroom,
        a tawdry chamber
                with its mattress
                        on the floor
                                mid candle spatters

and a blue print of Sappho's
        face, large as the wall,
                above the bed

"Now you shall learn
        the Rubbing of Oils
                & Glossa Didacta."


        Retentia
appeared at the door
    bearing a tray of
    tiny canopic jars

—oils & ungents
with which Sapph'

could ply her hands

       as she slid the
    clothing from shy John Barrett's
skinny frame
       & rubbed him thrillsomely
    from jar upon jar
       each oil having
    a different thrill
         —a mild sting here
           and a tremble there—

    & sweet smells
         mixing with
    smells piquant

"There is much you do not
know,"
     spoke she,
neatly hanging her peplos
upon a nail on the door
after she had shut it

She drew Barret down
O Barrett come down

"We have called it
    the Glossa Didacta
and every bard must have
      its perfect knowledge"

Down sank they
    upon J. Barrett's mattress

She pulled his poorly combed
                         badly washed curls
down upon the only thing substantial
          It was like a softened rosehip
          The rest of her was ghost-mist

          "Your head is the rudder
          & I shall steer it over
                         the rapids,"

      this way
          that way
      steering with fondly grabbed ears
      steering the rose bud
      steering the bard boy's brow

      showing him pressures
                         motions
                              patterns

       "That's it
        That's the way
        That's perfect"

    clitoris bifurcated
            like
            a
            lithops
  (left side to the right brain
  right side to the left brain?

            twain
            bundle
            of come-nerves?)

Lithops bella

She came in words arcane,
Sapph'-sighs writhing above her
in jumbles of
                    hieroglyphic neon,
        as when she had sung-—

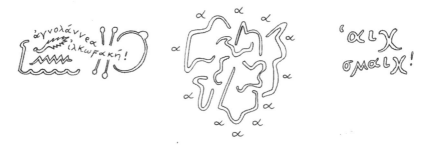

She spoke to him in Latin,
"Now I have taught you
                the Lingus Didacticus
and those you coax
                into its trembly thrall
shall know a dance more lightly tapped
than the meters of Euripides."

Then she bade him
                come inside her.

"Don't you make it only with, uh, gunaikes?"
                        he replied, breaking into Greek.

She'd arranged chianti bottles
                    around the bed
                            with flickering candles within

Barrett looked up
            to see the shadow
                        of the ghost
against her blue print image
                        on the wall
as she tugged him gently
                    but insistently
till they lay
            face to face
& she guided him up & within—

an hour
        to make him
                believe anew in the
                        thought of the Numen
or an hour
        as a catalpa blossom
                    floating in the River Thrill.

                Ahh, *côte-à-côte*
                he longed to lie
                with her
                upon the dawn—

        "Stand up," she said instead,
        "We're going on a journey."

        "If so," replied John Barrett,
        "give me satyr legs!
        yes, sturdy hairy legs
                    & hircine hooves
        to spring and leap!"

Sappho smiled, but
could not comply.
She held his hand

& floated
from the room on East 7th

above the green copse of
                Tompkins Park

dizzily dizzily
whirling a further era back—

to 1911
where Emma Hardy sat alone
on a spring morn
            at Max Gate*
her husband downstairs
correcting
        proofs
                with his mistress.

They entered Emma's bedroom
through the dormer windows
There was a feeding station
             by the sill
                  for the birds

Sappho felt pity
        for bitter Emma Hardy
                whose husband's hands

were ever poised
        to trace the
                curves of youth.

She was trying
        to ready herself
                for the day

* Max Gate—Thomas & Emma Hardy's house in East Dorset, Dorchester. In 1908 Emma had ordered dormer windows built in her attic boudoir, outside of which the birds at the feeding table would flock to eat from her hands.

but her face
       was twisted in pain
             from a torturing back

The pain was too consuming
       for her to lift
           a plate of crusts
               to the birds

She rang for her helper, Dolly Gale,
to brush her hair
Dolly stood behind her
       unbraiding  untangling  uncoiling
          the sleep-jammed tresses

The slightest tug
       of the bristles
          brought agony's gasp

till Sappho reached out
       to place a soothing palm
             on Emma's spine

       to ease away
       the axing ache

"The oil, John, the oil," Sapph' urged
and John Barrett parted the robe
           from the painéd shoulders

and began to caress
       with Mytilene's finest
          from a thin necked jar.

The peace in her back
       brought the first smile
            in months

"Call the birds for us, please Emma?"
Sappho asked, and Emma Hardy

walked to the sill
and raised her hands

Emma was 68
Emma in pain
Emma threw open the dormer
to feed them her wedding train

There must have been a hundred birds
in a wild gustation of feathery blurrs
above the feeding station
pecking the breakfast crumbs

"This house Hardy built," Sappho said to
John, with a tone of disgust,

"without a hot
water tub!"

She took his hand again— "Prepare for a trip
to 642 A.D."

There was a further whirling
after which
they alighted
at a site of steam & fire

Barrett thought for a moment
they might have followed
Dante and Vergil
into a bolge of hell

There was a hairless man
with a shiny skull
& a missing tooth in front

throwing bundles of papyrus
scrolls
into the wordeating mouth
of an open-hearthed ceramic furnace

Water boils above it
              in a large copper basin,
feeding through ducts to a
                   series of copper tanks
of varying stages of heat
so that a bather in
the pool can tug a string
for the heat of her choice.

Stacks of scrolls
           jut this way and that.
Barrett cranes his head
            to read the names
                   upon the next thatch
                              to be tossed

Oh, no! It takes a few seconds
              reading the run-on script
                     for John to recognize
                            the plays of Aeschylus!

    They are heating the baths of
    Alexandria
    with the last of the ancient
    libraries

"Look!" she cried, "Do you know what that is?"
The attendant had an armload of volumes*
with projecting knobs. "He's just about to burn
the final set of my collected works."

    The fireman
    tossed them two by two in the fameless flame

    Barrett tried to grab them
    but his hands brushed through
    like mist into a redwood bough

* Volume, from volumen, papyrus rolled around a stick or sticks, the text
  written in narrow columns.

"Some of my poems were
torched by Caesar
burning the ships in
Alexandria's bay
        & the fire reached ashore

Some were chopped into
papier-mâché for the
middle-class coffins of Thebes

Some were destroyed
when surly Christians
sacked the Serapeum*
in 391

And now it is time
for ashes and chars
to come to the
        mixolydian mode

Some poets' words
are written on water
Others make flame
        to make it moil."

Just then
    the voices of women
        & the clack of clogs
            were heard
  The daughter of General Amrou**
        had come  to soak
           in the steam-topped pool
& to smooth
    with pumice bars and strigils***
        their steam-soft skin

---

    *   one of the two ancient archives in Alexandria
  **  Amrou seized Alexandria for the caliph Omar in 642. The latter, it is said,
       ordered the remaining books in the ancient library destroyed on the grounds
       that now that the Koran had been written, they were no longer needed.
 ***  curved scrapers for removing bath-softened skin

The women
        passed their towels
                to their servants
and the high-domed room
                was soon resounding
                        with laughter and aqueous splash

All of a sudden Sapph' shoved past
                the sweaty man by the furnace
and gathered the final rolls,
                to Barrett's gasp,
        and flicked them into the rage

She turned, disrobed,
handed her chiton to
                Barrett
and slid into the water
to sit on a marble plank
                with the damozels
                in the moil pool's midst

"Hotter, hotter," she urged
the attendant, tugging on the rope
to empty a torrid tank
                upon them

                while out of the furnace
                a burning fragment fluttered

                just a corner of paper,
                        curling & burning

with Sapph's last word

βρενθεῖ῀ω

flaming

βρενθεῖ῀ω

It fell at Barrett's feet
He tried to stamp
      at the fire

    to no avail

A silver knob
    from the end of a scroll stick,
worked in a pattern of porpoises,
          rolled out of the furnace
    all that remained
  of the works
of Sappho of Mitylene

Barrett reached down to seize it
          He slipped
              & smashed to the floor.

He came awake
      in his pad on East 7th
and saw a foot on
      the fire escape.

"Sappho!" he half screamed,
      and rushed to the window

but it was Consuela
        in her Orchard St. chiton and peplos

She seemed asleep
        but opened her eyes at once
                when he touched her

She told him her tale
He told her his

showed her
the silver knob

and the smell of the top of his wrist
              still thrillsome
with Sappho's oil.

        Afraid, yet
            unable not, to
                talk about
           it

        Barrett told portions
        to some, &
        the whole event
        to a few
        with the silver knob
        as carefully shown
        as a saint's bone.

        To some
           he was
              Crazy John
("You sure this wasn't
        the head from your
              grandfather's cane?"
                Sam Thoma sneered)

To others
        he was
                Lucky Bard
(to carve the proper lyre
        to sing Sappho down
                Sappho come down)

Though he sang her each eve
he saw her no more
till early next year
on a snowy night

John saw Sappho
her neck laden
with heavy
Russian crosses

praying in the deep drift snow
on Avenue A

before it was disturbed
by salt & sweep

outside the redbrick
St. Nicholas
        Carpatho Russian
church

Icons were
melting in
her hands

& rubies
dropped
from her
crusted neck
into the snow

(though later
      they vanished)

He ran to see her
She was weeping

      "You'll cry too,"
        was all that she said

& she walked
away into the blizzard
weeping & wailing

& Barrett
never saw her again.

## Adios Diamond Sutra

Just a few
days after
the universe

began to implode,
the connoisseur
of mystic rubrics

looked back
as best he could
through the time-gasm

said "Adios
Diamond
Sutra"

## STAND BY MY SIDE,
## O LORD


So many people have been spoiled Vast Galaxies
It's hard to figure out
where to start
                  to study the lives
                  of the hieroglyphic
                  artists, literally,
                  ha

                        ha
                        how they lived
                        what studious
                        dumbness they plowed with
                        their fingers


        for what?    better to follow
        a curve
                        of mathematics
                                curlecues
                                        of madness
                        in a hall of shudders,
                        perhaps—


                                or was it better
                                at the end to
                                have followed the
                                advice of ancient forefathers?


        Through our technocracy
        & doodling in the genetic spew
        we try to Emanate
        & take our species
        onward into the house
        of the Lord—

        Is that what the message is?

The coronellae
        or th' space-ship helmets
                    on the petroglyphs
are not from space
but from    the inner eye-spray
of the dumplings
who stood to try
to raise
    a whisper
    into the rotting
    gravity of
    softsadness.

    Grabbst 'ou where I'm coming from,
    muh fuh?

When she didn't
like me, I didn't like
                me
She loved me later,
        & I fell apart.

Now I pray to be whole & gentle
grace-fingers raised up
like wheat
            for the bread of
            the void of paradise


            —1973

## Sun Arms

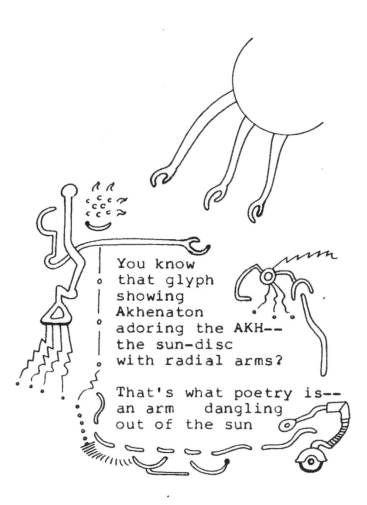

You know
that glyph
showing
Akhenaton
adoring the AKH--
the sun-disc
with radial arms?

That's what poetry is--
an arm     dangling
out of the sun

# Egyptian Hieroglyphs

*A Study of Rebels in Ancient Egypt*

# Egyptian Hieroglyphs:
## A Study of Rebels in Ancient Egypt

My mentor Charles Olson created a "Curriculum of the Soul" for which around 28 of his friends wrote fascicles—small books on subjects such as "Dream," "Blake," "the Norse," "Dante," "Alchemy," "Vision," and others. My assignment was "Egyptian Hieroglyhs." I spent months in 1973 researching Egyptian culture at the New York Public Library, looking for evidence of rebellious artistic generations about 2,000–1,500 B.C. along the Nile. Also, I studied facsimiles of the Mythological Papyri—beautiful painted scroll-like depictions of post-life voyages through the netherworld, plus books on Egyptian burial practices and ceremonies, so as to be able, for instance, to write of the burial and afterlife of the dancer Her-Wetet.

•Ab-Mer, a Love Story of 1985 B.C.

•Hieroglyphics

•I Want to be Purified

•The Singer

•Booty

•Report: Council of Eye-Forms Data Squad

•20,000 A.D.

## Ab-Mer

Hathor's farm and school of every art
had a fine broad lake
square as perfection
cornered by the finest Acacia trees
the breasts of Isis
hung from the branches

The gardens and orchards of Hathor's House of Life
moiled with abundance, the flocks
of animals grew like the seed of Ptah
under the urging of Hathor

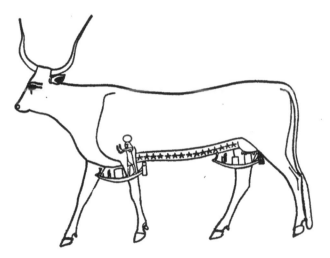

How many hundred-weights of honey
lay stored within the House of Hathor,
Countless, the bees of Hathor buzzed within the long reed hives
and poets writing lyrics walked blossom'd acres

So what if the quarter-mile wall
around the House of Hathor was rather in need of repair?
What midget from the
robber camps in the marshes

would climb up over to steal?
What jewels were there to
steal from the House of Hathor?
What thief would want
long poems on parchment?
What could he get for that? since
Limited Signed Editions were 1000s of years away.

What was the price of sketches
on old wine casks?
No robber after gold
or red stones would bother
when the graves of the desert
held tons of wealth.

Soldiers patrolling the wasteland temples of wealthy dead
with long-snouted dogs on leash
whispered how displeased the vizir's agents were
with Hathor's Rebel House of Life.

By the standards of the time, 1985 B.C.
in the beginning of the first of the
Middle Kingdom dynasties, it was a small House of Life,
but self-sufficient,
collecting to its walls the finest painters, dancers,
singers, poets, musicians, stone workers, wine makers
and tasters of the above, rebels all, full of energy
and full of love of Hathor and Hathor's whispered 'joinder to Ra:
"Part thy robes, O Ra, and we shall conjoin."

. Ready were the artists of Hathor to fill the valley Nile
with beatnik potsherds, Hathor lore, papyri drawn with visions
never seen beneath the deity-clogged skies of overarching Nut.

Nothing sang as sweet
as Hathor's singers
No one could raise the skin
and the scatter-dance of love
so far into the heights
as Hathor's singers

What a school of singers was the House of Hathor

    None could draw with
    such consummate skill
             as the draughtsmen of Hathor
    No one could raise such thunderous anger
    from petty clerks in the civil government
             as the draughtsmen of Hathor

    and the poets raised up such a complete complex
    of derision and anger:

  "Put trivia upon the basalt blocks. It's
    better than lists of captive slaves" was sort
    of the motto of the House
    which caused the court-creeps to rail with anger, urged the King
    to snuff out "those uppity scratchers."

What a school of art and verse, The House of Hathor

    Nor could any pluck the harp
    or beat upon a row of drums
    or pick with gentle squalls of notes
    'pon the nefer-guitar
    like the women & men there dwelling

What a school of music and drum, The House of Life of Hathor

        Beer was sacred to Hathor
        and every revel
        save that of Apep.

        And ahh the beer
        produced by the artists
        of Hathor

        sweet with dates
            the beer grew
            within the
            barley dough

& the wine dripped lascivious
out of the press
best in the land.

Grumbles and whispers
swept the land con-
cerning the rites of Hathor
held in the House of Life.

All night long they drank
the sacred drool
All night long
the household danced for Hathor
who raised her skirt for angry Ra,
Hathor of the Horns.

The drummers incomparable and
twin-reed flutists urged the swirling,
the dancers shook the sistra
they shook the square tambourines
they clacked the ivory finger-cymbals
& Hathor of the Sycamores
walked toward Ra, and Ra sent
barques of servants underneath
to touch the stars of Hathor.
o rites of Hathor.

Meanwhile
Ammenemes I 1991–1962
beginning of the 12th dynasty
transferred many artists down the
Nile from the area of Thebes to
Memphis, and notice was served upon
The House of Life of Hathor
to get ready to hit the bricks.

No one at the House of Hathor
wanted to leave sweet Thebes
for Memphis merely to cop
a scope on the "great Art of the

past"
just because some jacked-off jackal
of a King desired to push their
minds, therefore their art, therefore
their muscles 4/5/600 years back
to 2600 B.C.

Ab-Mer was an artist lived
at Hathor's House of Life
Ab-Mer the painter/carver

And Ab-Mer was sorely angered
by the Pharaoh.
When he was
                    alone
                    he shouted
                    the King's name

He threw crocodile dung
at the sun shouting
"The worm eat the King!"

Then, curse upon curse,
Ab-Mer was fired from
his job as coffin-carver
for the royal snuff-works
for drawing
a weirdo version
of the King's cartouche
upon a fresh pine box,
drew an ear
where the sun-disk
should have been.
"Son of Ear!" his friends laughed
in the tented saloon,

"Here's a drink
to getting fired
for the carving
of the King's ear!!"

"A fist upon the King!"
"Hathor!" and all drank
and dancing the poets sang.

The sin of the writers, musicians,
dancers, painters, stone workers, &
"tasters of combinations" as some
were known who partook of several
skills—the sin in the authorities'
mind was that the House of Hathor
extended all such deific protection
from the kings and queens and
courtoids to all the people,
especially those at the Hathor
House of Life.

"We are the glyphs
    we are the people dancing
    we are the magic colors
        upon the graven cedar planks
    we are the writers we are the
        curls of the melons of the
        gardens
    we are the people singing and
        singing on paper
    we ARE the ceremonies!"—
this was their attitude.
"The grain belongs to everybody"—
passed about on pot-pieces
for those who could read.

When Ab-Mer cursed the Pharaoh,
as common to any police state
the word drifted up the power-
climb adorned with grotesque
additions—The King was
afraid of the curse. What insolent
carver of coffins dared
trash the King!? It will be noted
that the Pharaoh did wear a cobraic

uraeus on a hippie headband 'pon his
mantled brow which was designed
to handle and to ward off the
oncoming vibes of destruction. But,

like kings of all times he never
quite trusted his defenses.
So he put out a contract for the
brick-out of Ab-Mer the caustic
carver, with a team of scowling
crude robbers of graves in a
tent town deep in marshes
south in Upper Egypt.

While the goons were floating
down the Nile, Ab-Mer was singing
w/ menandwomen friends, passing
a paper roll by the cool lake
in the closed court-grove on
grounds of the House of Hathor,
upon which roll they all
were composing a satire-skit
about the King.

Moans of eager skin
leaked forth till a sword hooked
into the side of the tent
and the rude King's hit-men
started to chop, shouting
            "Where is Ab-Mer?"
"Ab-Mer we cut up your face?"—bodies
dashing in the garden
whence Ab-Mer somehow escaped, formulae
of hatred
boiling upon his lips.

Late at night Ab-Mer
sneaked back into the compound
to dance with I-mm-eti
the love of his life.

She wore a small stone Ab-Mer painted
with her portrait

as she shook.
He watched her dance, he danced also
and all the sistra-shakers, drummers
quitar-players surging for Hathor

I-mm-eti dipped back down
upon the dance platform
back bend, shimmy,
back bend

Ab-Mer loved the one who danced
there more than his heart
could bear
            almost.

And when their eyes met
eyes danced out of the sockets
and the eyes took off the eye-clothes
and one eye drew atop the other
and the eye-tongue slid upon the shiny eye.

Late late the chorus of Hathor sang
as I-mm-eti swayed and shimmied
bounced and leaped into exhaustion.

But after 15 minutes rest
the frazzle turned to frenzy
and torrid need
o'erwhelmed them.

I-mm-eti nodded him come to her rooms
where shards of his drawings ringed the walls
and poems they wrote made love upon the plaster.

And not since Isis taking the form of a bird
did hover above Osiris
to take him within
did such a love convulse upon the Nile
as I-mm-eti and Ab-Mer the outlaw
throughout the nighttime found Hathor
's wild flood
drowning the tramples of the spear-men
searching the marshes for Ab-Mer
cursed the Pharaoh.

But morning found the laughter of Hathor twisted to groan
and doomed with separation, danger, dread of death
Ab-Mer slipped down the Nile, through the Delta, and off
to an island, crying every day for years and years
but losing the grasp of the love lost tragic.

And I-mm-eti made a mistake
one night drunk on henek, the barley beer,
and the child grew within
and she was seized enslaved by a mean man
who smelled of burnt goose-feathers
for a life of never a dance.

Ab-Mer was able to return from exile 20 years later
during the senility of King Ammenemes 1
but could not find his love

though he searched from cottage to tent to hut to house
both sides of the river
but no one knew her, remembered her, or thought to find.

And as for the Risen House of Hathor—
when Ab-Mer returned it was many years
since the great fire wiped that down into the
sand    and the great art lay beneath the claws of
the griffin vultures.

And Ab-Mer secured a position
in another House of Life, more sedate
more powerful, wealthy, modest
where Ab-Mer became a staid bent disciple
of rectitude. "I lost my chops,"
he'd moan beneath a load of
wine, railing against the Nile-side water stick
forboding drought.

The aged drunken Ab-Mer
lowered his weeping face to the table.

Then
"Hathor!" he cried, "Hathor
I shall dance!" and
the old man
rose to dance, and dancing
tore some sinews
in his legs and
stumbled to the flooor where
purple bruises spread
beneath his dry barked skn.

"I-mm-eti" whispered Ab-Mer
"o I-mm-eti."

# Hieroglyphs

Each word a
flash-pod correspondent
to an event
in the Great Beyond
or the Yaru Fields
as in the
possibility of Coming Forth by Day

the hiero-symbol

Keep that grain
swooning
Hathor, please!

THANATOIDAL
TRANSFORMATION
EQUATIONS

"Thou comst out of thy grave every morning
Thou returnst every evening
Thou passest through eternity in pleasure"

by the living swarmies
painted on papyrus

by the hiero-symbols
painted 'pon basalt
to        the Beyond

soul scroll

in a box
wrapped
in the mummy cloth
or stuck into the coffin

believing that
the words
and pictures

would insure transreal
grooviness for the snuffee

No greater belief in
words has there been

## I Want to Be Purified

I want
to be purified
in the

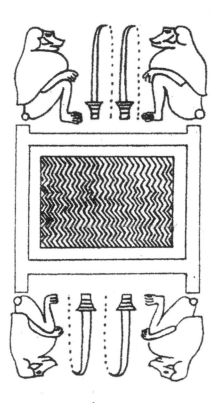

she sang

# The Singer

The blind harp-strummer
sat before the vizir's banquet
singing of shrieks and shrieks
and thoughts of shrieks and symbol shrieks
and new shrieks bouncing surly
down upon the faded shrieks of faded pain

"Hang garlands on the neck of your wife
and garlands on her arms,

and listen overhead"—sang the blind Egyptian harper
"and listen underfoot
and sing when there is silence
and sing when there is safety
and sing sing sing"

While 4,600 years later
there once was a singer

and a writer of songs
who worked in a bar far off
near Blabtos, Georgia

The week was up and the singer walked
into the office of the club
collecting he hoped the rest of his
pay

which had to be given him
all in cash
according to the terms of his contract
with the club

The owner looked askance
at the tired grimy person of tunes, he
snorted down from his nose just as
he hooted smoke from his mouth
and the grey boiled downward, disappeared

The sheriff's been
looking at the wheels
of your van and they
don't look none too safe

Besides you sing
ugly, little man
your band belongs
in a high school basement

We reckon a hundred dollars
and a free trip out of town
ought to do you right good.

But you owe me 300 dollars!
Sweat was breaking out upon his long
black sideburns

& his eyes were wide with piss-off
sweat too spread over his blue satin shirt

wherever there was hair beneath

And the band's got to get their pay
Mr. Parsons!

           No mind to me
           son, he replied
           I don' give no frig
           for those tub thumps
           call themselves a band

           But those hundreds of folk
           who came! What about
           them?  Hunh! My customers
           come for to guzzle
           boy, don' forget it
           guzzle! guzzle!
           Now take this hundred
           and get    and don't
           go howling to my cousin
           over at the union
           neither.

Sheriff! He's in here
givin' me some lip.
And watch your badmouthing me
hear?

           I ain't going out of here
           till you 'fill the terms
           of my contract. He pulled
           the wadded wet-with-sweat document
           out of his back pocket
           unfolded it & held it
           up to the light—I'll have to sue

Give me that! the owner snarled
and grabbed it out of his hand
tore it shreds

The singer
knocked the owner down
locked him
shirt pulled up his back
saw the white kidney—
twinge of evil, singer couldn't
stop his hand    hack the
fatty mountain—aiee! the
head of the owner flipped back and forth
lips slobber pain.
Help! Murder . . . kidneys! Sheriff!

The sheriff banged open the
door    door-edge thudded
the singer's side
He pulled them apart    then clubbed
the singer with the gun-butt

thomp! thomp! Goddamn greasy
little pretender. Why don't you
get a haircut? I heard you, off-color songs
mixed up w/ church songs. You got
no right to put on an act like that.
Mr. Parsons's right to pay you what
you deserve

Now get on out of here
in that van of illegality
you call a home—

And the sheriff
pushed him
staggering for balance out of
the club, past the sweepers bent
in the sawdust, into the
alley.

With sounds of ptuh! ptuh!
he sputtered the blood from his lips
and started the engine

then let the steel guitar player drive
when he got the urge to sing
and crawled into the back of the van
where he pulled a guitar off the wall
and sang almost till dawn
when the van pulled up at
a motel near the Tennessee border

# Booty

Like a dog-breathed homunculus
the wizened child crawled along
the cedar sluice

       squeaky rumbled the dyspeptic colon
       and no wonder so
       for they froze the growth
       kept the boy like a monkey
       fed vulture scraps

      "Gotta keep lil Mek-mok small"
      quoth dad.

The cedar plank-tongue
slowly had slid     150 feet    through Princess Her-Wetet's
mountain tunnel
not touching any sides or floor    lest the trigger
tumble the mntn liths

His father, older brother, grandpa
waited at the sunlight
for the child to load the booty upon the sluice-sledge

Fruition! Fruition! the grandpa rubbed his hands in glee

      "We will
        pull out the plank
        the little brat
        will try to run
        out toward us, then . . ."

For 75 years the robber clan of Mek-Macrae
had tried to crawl

through Her-Wetet's smooth straight tunnel
into the Theban mountain

but the designer had fiendishly
set traps at regular spots
on the walls and ceiling and floor
so that a light, passing foot, or pressure on the wall would
trigger an avalanche of adios,
tons of the mountain.

Mek-mok the boy had lost his uncle
and uncle's uncle two different times
they tried—dead in crush-liths.

The Tomb of Princess Her-Wetet,
Chantress of Amon:

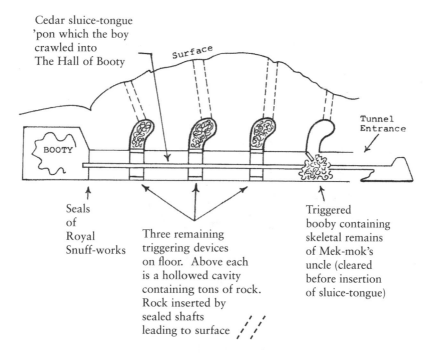

Cedar sluice-tongue
'pon which the boy
crawled into
The Hall of Booty

Surface

BOOTY

Tunnel
Entrance

Seals
of
Royal
Snuff-works

Three remaining
triggering devices
on floor. Above each
is a hollowed cavity
containing tons of rock.
Rock inserted by
sealed shafts
leading to surface

Triggered
booby containing
skeletal remains
of Mek-mok's
uncle (cleared
before insertion
of sluice-tongue)

The finest    Lebanese planks
built end to end
like a medical spatula
for some huge deity such as Ptah

with sides built
up with edging
(prevent the sledge
full of looting
          fall off the tongue
          trigger any rock-plop)


The boy crept through the murk with
tallow torches
                    toward the moolah
along the well-oiled sluice
dragging the small sledge
150 feet of rope off either end.


    Mek-mok slowly loaded the satchels
    from the treasure room of Her-Wetet's tomb
    upon the sledge
    and the robbers at the entrance pulled
    it to the light
    then Mek-mok reeled the empty back for reload.

←————— rope ——— [sledge] ——— rope —————→


    The boy was (slightly) daffy
    smashed a miniature granary
    with a ceremonial oar
                    disturbed vibes
                    upsetting the Princess
                    by means of those
    THANATOIDAL TRANSFORMATION EQUATIONS


                    as she was plucking 'ternal wheat
                    down on Paradise Farm

    The Nubian reapers
    bent in Yaru pleasure alongside the Princess
                    just as the boy was chopping up the tomb

fell down groaning
their mer-cutters splaying
        princess bent in agony

Robbers didn't care, they
sought the jewels, the gold
and yes     the precious oils

Mek-mok was sloppy
oil jugs rolled off the sluice
smashed

        one in particular indicating
        that the Princess had been burned
        by the Regal Purveyor of scents—
        not oil, but ooze unholy
        village struck by flash-plague
        such stench

phew!
        eyes smarting, nose like snorting
        ground-up brillo pad.

Mek-mok ice-picked the rubies from
the statues of the Princess

        A scream of pain
        in the grain fields of Heaven
        "My eyes! my eyes!" red pits
        where eyes had.

        Transformation     transformation

"Canst 'ou see now
in the Yaru River bottoms
Princess dear? "Nyuf hyuf hyuf" im-
portuned the griseous-fingered thiefboy

pried the gold leaf off
the coffin sledge, broke the alabaster jars

dry friable guts of Her-Wetet
spilling on the row of sacred oars.

The rob-boy stuck    a couple of gold wheat-stalks
into his mouth, thinking of fangs
laughed,  "look at me!   look at me!"

Will Her-Wetet walk a pauper through Elysium?
Forever adrift
                in a reed boat
reft of the total pleasure
promised by the words of the walls
down upon the howling banks of
the

# RIVER

# Report:
## Council of Eye-Forms Data Squad

DATA!    DATA!

| | |
|---|---|
| Subject: | Her-Wetet<br>Chantress of Amon |
| Case File: | Dimension $X°_{147}$_44739J |
| Time: | 1153 B.C. |
| Place: | Necropolis, Thebes, Egypt |

Subject was a Female Hamitic, 5'11" Bl/Br approx. 140 lbs. age 37—cause of death: stampede of hippopotami. This writer attended various nodules of the embalming ceremonies. Subject was afforded a full 70-day spice-douse wherein subject's features were held remarkably intact.

A report of the Yaru Surveillance Team is attached below as <u>Appendix A.</u>

Imposition of the Nether Glyph ( ⊕ ) occurred in 70 days.

During this period the coffins and artifacts were carved and painted. The texts of the Book of the Dead 'dorned with the fair *beauté* of Her-Wetet torrid chantress, were drawn up in 7 colors 'pon the wide papyrus scroll.

70 days to ⊕

Brain was hooked out through nose
    some of it dissolved via dissolve-gush poured within
        brain thrown away, no care fo' rotting data files
      heavy chop scene
        performed on bod

guts disgorged    mummified    placed

liver    lungs    tum    intestines
                    tum

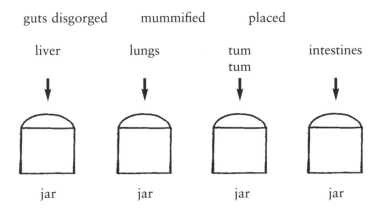

jar    jar    jar    jar

    in graven alabaster
    protected by the 4 sons of Horus

    these canopic containers put
    upon a sacred sledge

post scrape-job re inner mush gush
cavity packed with pieces of natron salt
(sodium carbonate  sodium bicarbonate
sodium chloride    sodium sulphate)
wrapped in linen
        suck up body ooze
          body drool
natron sprinkled on the outer also
—dry Egyptian climate helped the dry-out

After the jerkification, natron removed
body given water sponge bath
then rub-a-dubbed with resins coniferous
cavities packed with resin-soaked wads o' linen
—stuffed with taxidermist's care: "life! life!"

Stan Brakhage, Eye-Form Surveillance data-positor
filmed the sew-up
stone eye
        placed on chop-scar
        prior to the long winding

fingers, toes
wrapped separately
toe-stalls   finger-stalls
of gold
        coatings of resins
        applied to coatings of linen
        175 yards of linen strips used
        to wrap the subject chantress
        Her-Wetet.

           There was a slight
           but saveable error
           —portion of the right ear
           was discovered beneath
           the chop bench
           swept up, according to the
           ceremony, with the spilt
           desiccative and linen pieces extra,
           buried in the storage jars
           near the mouth of her tunnel.

By barge procession
passed
right bank to left bank, Nile
down into the Valley of Salient Snuff

oxen pulled
the sledge

           mourners fisted dirt in poofs
           self-beat, shrieks
           & long dinny moans

friends of Her-Wetet, plus

priests and servants
and porters with platters
of gifts.

> By the edge of the tunnel
> last ceremony
> coffin
> tipped on its end
>
> "opening of the mouth"
> that the chantress
> yodel gently
> down where the scoffers
> cannot scoff

Priest in role as Deity
drove out the
devil dirt, like

> "out thou ⌐ꓝꓼꓸꓼ -fiends
> out thou hitler verbs
> out moloch out nixon out
> of this voice!"

### APPENDIX A.

Eye-Form Surveillance Team
was required to utilize
Beckmanian
Transformation Nodes (via diagonal dimension dives)

in order       to hover behind
The Death Barque      while
still escaping the particularly wary wet-fanged
                              attendant Deity known as
Anubis

The jackaline Anubis
is thought to be able to undertake a nearly N-
dimensional scientia-sweep
so it was necessary to observe only from

those dimensions he was unable to fathom.

Her-Wetet, The Chantress of Amon, was observed
in the rapids of showery rubicund petals just prior
to being sucked into the golden eyeball wherein the
petal torrent falls and disappears. It is stunningly
beautiful to see the soul-brain fall through the Eye.

Dimensional Adjustment Procedures enabled the
Eye-Form Surveillance Team to observe the Princess
arriving in the first sections of The Underworld.

When the rope of the Ferry was thrown ashore
a cat-headed goddess (holding a whip) led the singer
toward and through the so-called Door of Percipience

Hallelujah
       the deceased     strolled quietly past
       42 fierce Spiritual Assessors

       Soul-jewel shining
                no sin-grime cloying
                            Hallelujah

       Osiris reached in between her breasts
       and brought out her heart

       Jackal-headed Anubis
       lifted her heart
              upon the scales
              heart on one tray
              against the Maat feather
              on the other

              Little baboon jumping
              up and down on the mid pole

              while Ibis-headed Thoth   wrote down
              the data on a tablet

Concomitant with the weighing
was the chanted enumeration of sins <u>not</u>
committed


(If th' accumulated sin-grime didn't tilt the
heart against the Feather then

Heaven!
but if it tilted, then soul, and it is confusing
here, would either   a)   be doomed to roam Earth
                               b)   be consigned to the fiends of
                                     Adios Chew Devour
                                     the so-called 𓂋𓊪𓄿𓃥 -fiends
                               c)   be eaten by a low slung
                                     wrinkle-snouted Devourer
                                     known as Am-Mut
                               d)   all of the above.)


Blameless in truthful blessèd bliss-out surged
the sinless Chantress of Amon when her heart
balanced the Maat

Osiris tucked it back within
her bounteous bosom

And the low slung
wrinkle-snouted slime gobbler Am-Mut
had to wait for ano'r time ano'r soul
to suck from the plate of truth.



Subject chantress then endured the marvel of The Final Purification
in the Lake of Fire

guarded by 4 apes holding torches—


4 torches extinguished
in the 4 pails
of Universal Milk . . .

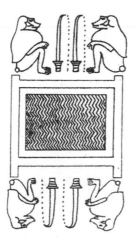

It is to be noted here
that ALL this judgement was hard indeed to
bring to surveillance:

Shifting Forms . . .
unable to
jot them
as they shift . . .
Dream-Stream
film just blurs:

What is she doing? The subject Chantress and baboon
 of Thoth adore the Solar Disk

No! No! Dummy! The subject Chantress is actually
 bowing down before the supine
 Deity: Crocodile Earth

Bull Shit! The subject Chantress is being led
 by the triune Ptah-Osiris-Sokaris
 for induction into the Mysteries

Hear the chant of the priests: "That she may
make all the transformations she desires"

Forms    Forms    Forms    Forms
Apparently jubilant over her new abilities
subject assumed a razzle-dazzle arpeggio
of weird forms:
>microbe, heron, swallow, ox
>mollusk, rain storm, church
>steeple, projective verse
>what a dazzling sequence!

And more:  subject Her-Wetet on Ra-raft
>subject Her-Wetet as Sky Bug
>then Ra-Hawk    Solar Disk
>Sun Flower    Cherry Blossom

She might have volunteered for a tour
of duty as an oarsperson
on the Solar Barque
>>but one of the strangenesses
>>of this particular paradise
>>is that they settle down, the souls,
>>to reap bright grain in a
>>brass-walled place
>>called The Yaru Fields

>where the Spirits are precisely  10'6" tall
>where the grains are precisely  10'6" tall
>and the grain-ears precisely  3 feet long

>said fields
>located in the 2nd Arit (or Mansion)
>of the 7 Arits
>>Underworld.

Accordingly, Her-Wetet settled down to a normal death
and walked toward Yaru.

There are twin sycamores
of malachite at the world's end
twixt which
>Ra oozes forth

There is the Western Mntn
where Hathor Cow
goddess of necropolis

met the snuffee
saying "Hi!
the grain field's that way!"

Image shift: celestial bull and 7 kine
4 rudders of He'v'n
Shu muscling Nut off Geb

"Hi, Hathor!" as the soul of Her-Wetet
beaconed in thrillsome shifting tides
of form and form

Then Her-Wetet happ'ed to walk past
godly Osiris lying on his back
on the loamy mount of Khepri

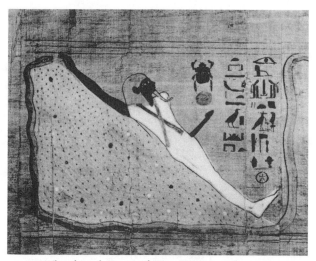

The festal cone of Her-Wetet melts
in the fire of their pleasure
Her-Wetet atop the god
belly burning

Subject chantress was not hesitant in fact frequently
to interrupt her wheat-cutting activities in the eons
thereafter and to run over to Khepri Mountain
and to effect unification with the Deity known as
Osiris (a Male Black, about 19'6", weight approx. 430 lbs.,
with extremely bloodshot, maybe entirely rubicund, eyes;
wearing blue beard and blue wig; armed with flagellum)

Scarcely had subject
begun to work in the
sun wheat when subject
bent over   as if in pain
her eyes   looked like
the insides of ketchup bottle caps

Subject winced—
The wheat field
where she and her
companions (unknown
Male Blacks wearing Nubian
wigs and armed with scythes)
were deep in harvest,
fell apart   in disarray.

> Dimensional Scan Operation
> indicated a forcible intrusion
> into her mountain tomb-tunnel
> by the robber clan known as
> the Mek-Macraes
> where certain stones were pried
> from votive statues, a
> model granary was beaten
> t' toothpicks therein.

Subject cantatrice rolled moaning down.
Her body bent
a long row of grain
with
        falling rolling
so that the sun-wheat heavy

struck muffled gong sound
against the Yaru Walls of brass.

Subject stumbled forth
along the River Bank

"My Eyes!    My Eyes!"

# 20,000 A.D.

The Council of Eye Forms
a liberal, nay even radical body of
intergalactic deities

composed itself upon various mutually agreeable
dimensions—namely those dimensions denigrated
by some, not in the Council of course, as "useless
Thrill-dimensions"—but nonetheless, a suitable
series of dimensions for communication among the
members of the Council of Eye Forms,

the purpose of the meeting being a general tactical
discussion of the aeon-long "Apopis problem"—
now that Apopis had apparently been caused to crumble
into desuetude in the so-called
                    "14th-emanation dungeon
                        of gutted phantoms."

In the texts
Apopis was always stun-stomped
but like
an angry maniac
or stare-at-me! psychopath
                strode/slithered
                forth   forever & a day
                to the boos and hisses
                of th' blobs
                of conscious molecules.

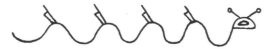

1) execration
2) sympathetic magic
                were the traditional rituals

by which the priests
paralyzed Snake
                at the "critical moment"
when Snake
                was going to
chew the lightnings and erg-sprays
off the sun
like a flower

                        to leave
                        a vermiform sky-ice
                        scene   for

                        the apparent purpose of
                        the self of him
                        to writhe in worship
                        of himself as the Total.

With a corona of fabricated TV broadcasts
a long eel in coils
of knife-stabbed red waves
upon the nadir of encroachment,

what a struggle, in lives & gore & misery
it was
        to tap those blades
                into the rolling back
                        of Apopis.

Accordingly, and be it remembered that this is just
a tale, The Council
held Snake 'neath the fierce administration of
                an N-dimensional
                        Milky Way- μῶλυ
                        or trance-moly.

Silence reigned where shrieks were once the revenue.
Drops could be heard
in the golden chalice

it was so silent
upon the belly of the
All.

But
the august sere angst-heads

debated
far too far into the "night"
the question of Apopis

e'en with the knowledge of so many trillions of ex-cons
(Council terms for the expansion/contraction of the Big)
when Worm rode berserk—

but now! lay stunned
within his current form of
    175,000 miles of starshine snakegrease.

Think upon it earthlings!
to rid the star-pelt all
of Apopine gore-gobble.

For a' that and a' that
the good Council
shed tears

        o'er the death-hacked Apopis

though Apopis
        spat hate
            & crests of destruction—

                "Each morn
                he tried to bushwhack
                the sun
                    arising in

                                        the arms
                                        of perfect love!" railed

                                                the prosecutor
                                                Eye Form.

But eve-time
found the Hate Worm—
knives in his back jangle/jiggling

                        ready to
                suck the yummy fires
                        of

And pray to know why the Council of Eye Forms
did hesitate to snuff forever
the vengeful, violent, remorseless

street-punk
                on the avenues
                        of the Universal Hole?

"Dost 'ou <u>really</u> really pine for Apep*
be a lawless field-fluid of crazed gravity?"

sang a languid Form nicknamed The Coma in
many a set of dimensions.

And many shuddered indeed at such a "thought."

Meanwhile the trance-moly waned.
And pity raised up the child of pity,
manumission.

* another name for Apopis

Turgid, then slowly warping
then faster faster faster

Apopis rolled, coil 'pon coil,
out of the dungeon
shrieked and cackled
farting clouds of revenge,

spitting a promise of Merry Pain-mass
to all the beasty bands of molecules

grown out of the nature of mad Sky
to stare and dare and be aware
beloved 'pon beloved.

# Why Hesitate
# to Know All
# Gentle Things

## The Thirty-Fourth Year

Today read *Steelwork* by Sorrentino
*100 Selected Poems* by e. e. c.
*The Metaphysical Poets*
      esp. Thomas Carew
      "An Elegie upon the Death of the Deane of Pauls,
      Dr. John Donne"

Made a list of letters to write,

        1)      2)
                     3)

        4)  5)  6)

Worked on 6 short stories.

To know that
mirth supplies divisions

To live as tense art
watch friends lie in a bathtub of blood

d.a. levy call his mother
      say he's going to go to S.F. work in the P.O.
      or maybe kill himself

      on the monuments

Dave Hazelton with whom canoe'd out to
confront Polaris submarines 1961
1968 came back fro Amsterdam
      saw him one day he lost his teeth
      jumped from the bridge gone the
      editor of *Synapse* Berkeley 1965.

So it's there
like an alphabetical file
of autopsy reports
can't face life like a fistfight
must crawl down lonely arroyos

Rain washes the rodents down the sluice
Fire wipes the Bronx

And to watch Richard Nixon
trying to summon pity as he goes
into the hospital, same room as Johnson
heart attack—probably wired w/ special
lines—a bedside red telephone
so that if he should suffer swiftly
maybe die, he could still phone in those
SAC's & minuteman missiles
squelch the world.

a)  to float along
b)  to become a dandy
c)  to practice as a scholar
d)  give up, get farm
e)  to prepare a list of books to
     write this decade, proceed
f)  push self toward ego dissolution, peace-in-practice,
     serve, lick stamps forever in a mailing
     room of protest bulletin
g)  bowery
h)  make movies only, or maybe write a 40-year
     opera/poem
i)  give up literature, write a manifesto about a
     new mode of painting, sneer, work hard on canvas,
     decorate space ships
j)  found a radical socialist quarterly—muckrake,
     poetics, sedition
k)  Phil Whalen: copy everything he does

—B'day
August 17, 1973

## For Paul

In 58 & 59
flesh out of Mo.
as a nascent beatling
cowering in the Café Figaro
    after Greek Class

reading *Beatitude*
and the early *Evergreen Review*s

one of my goals
was to meet Paul Blackburn
& to become his friend.

    It was a definite pleasure
    to purchase his
    early books

    *The Nets,*
   *& Brooklyn-Manhattan Transit*
        down in the
        superversepower basement of the 8th
    St. Bookshop.

And later there were the readings.

    He had such dedication
    to the spoken
    poem

      Who can forget the
      readings at the 10th St.
      Coffee House, at Les
      Deux Mégots, or at th'
      Le Métro Café

say 1964
ahh that such
peace of verse
should flow again
down 2nd Avenue
the cobbles

If you listened at all
in 1963
I bet you can still
hear his lines &
breaths  &  cadences

    I loved to hear him read

        you could <u>feel</u>
        <u>his line</u>

    The way he could chant
    with that deep base line
    almost like a held vowel
    underneath

        the words . . .

The way
he could
click open
his zippo lighter
as a punctuation
right in the middle
of a poem
        to light up a Picayune
      puffs pouring out of his mouth
    as further punctuation.

        He faced
        the terror
        it seemed to me
        with such tender grace.

I sometimes hear the
flashes of his conversation
filled with poesy's sunfolk—

say, how much awe he felt for the work
of Robert Kelly, and worried for his health

and the anecdotes, he told them with glee,
about the time one night, Tim Reynolds . . .

I remember he wrote a poem
celebrating someone who'd first turned him on
to Bols gin
   a few empty brown ceramic bottles of which
   sat on his windowsill
       attesting the thrill
  & he'd recommend it
         your way
    as gin-flash

   & he'd make sure
   you knew where to
 get some special coffee
     beans he knew about
      for that morning
     pre-verse  wire-up

    1964
    gave me
    directions how
    to locate
    some of those
    long thin
    notebooks
    in which he
    was writing
    his Bakery Poems

  an extraordinarily obscure
  little stationery store

                    up in the 20s
                    off Lexington Avenue.

        I can close my
        eyes & see him again
        19 E. 7th    his
        2nd floor apartment
        with those remarkable
        shiny sanded floors

        & in the back, his work room
        off the kitchen

        a long neat shelf of tapes
        above the desk

    He must have taped
                two hundred readings

        (    & yes the memories of sitting
                down at a table just about to read,
                to look nearby, hey!  there's Paul
                bent down near the floor, winding
                fresh tape upon the reel!   )

    And he <u>knew</u> his tape recordings:

                he'd tell
                you about
                some introduction
                you once made to a poem
                in a reading you'd long forgotten
                        & both you'd chuckle
                        afresh
                        again.
            & when you left his house
                    he always said, "Peace."

The problem is
that it's just too easy
to say something like
"the sad molecules convulse in the mist"

or that the supernova
supercedes—

·But they can't take
his voice away from us—
yes—I'll have hot cider
w/ a cinnamon stick—in
my mind again—
I can hear his voice
any time I want

It is late spring
1964

The tables are crowded
with nervous
poets clutching
their springbinders

the coffee costs too much

but the words are free

    Paul is reading
it is a good night

            and like a
            good percussionist
        the poet clicks open
            the lighter
            in the cadence.


—1974

# The Age

This is the Age of Investigation, and every citizen must
  investigate! For the pallid tracks of guilt and death,
  slight as they are, suffuse upon the retentive
  electromagnetic data-retrieval systems of our era.
  And let th' investigators not back away one micro-unit
  from their investigations—for the fascist hirelings
  of gore await in the darkness to shoot away the
  product of the ballot box

And if full millions do not investigate, we will see the
  Age of Gore, and the criminals of the right will rise up
  drooling with shellfish toxin, to send their berserker
  blitz of mod manchurian malefactors mumbling with
  motorized beowulfian trance-instructions, to chop
  up candidates in the name of some person-with-a-serotonin-
  imbalance's moan of national security

And this is the Age of Investigative Poetry, when verse-froth
  again will assume its prior role as a vehicle for the
  description of history—and this will be a golden era
  for the public performance of poetry: when the Diogenes
  Liberation Squadron of Strolling Troubadours and Muckrakers
  will roam through the citadels of America to sing
  opposition to the military hit men whose vision of the
  USA is a permanent War Caste & a coast-to-coast cancer
  farm & a withered, metal-backed hostile America forever

And this is the age of left-wing epics with happy endings! of
  left-wing tales / movies / poems / songs / tractata / manifestoes /
  epigrams / calligrammes / graffiti / neonics and Georges
  Braque frottage-collage-assemblage Data Clusters which
  dangle from their cliffs the purest lyricals e'er
  to hang down a hummingbird's singingbird throat

This is the age of Garbage (pronounced Garbájzhe).
  And we're not talking here about

Garbage Self-Garbage—but an era of robotic querulousness—
how at the onset of a time when the power of a country
is up for grabs, the Garbage Hurlers, attired in robes
of military-industrial silk, arise to hurl, as swift
in their machinations as a chorus in the Ice Capades:

and none of us will trudge this era without a smirch-face
waft of thrilly offal dumped upon our brows of social
zeal—and the pus-suck provocateurs armed with orbiting
plates of dog vomit will leap at us while we stand
chanting our clue-ridden dactyls of KNOW THE NEW FACTS
EARLY! Know-the-new-facts-early, know-the-new-facts
early! And do not back away one micro-unit just because
some CIA weirdomorph whose control agents never ended
WWII invades your life with a mouthful of curdled
exudate from the head of the Confederate Intelligence
Agency &

This is the Age of Nuclear Disarmament—when the roamers of
the Hills join hands with the nesters of the Valley
Wild, to put an end to nuke puke w/ a zero-waver total
transworld Peace Walk—that the War Caste wave no
more their wands of plutonium and the dirks
in the nuclear mists no longer chop up the code of life

And this is the Age of the Triumph of Beatnik Messages of Social
Foment Coded into the Clatter of the Mass Media over
20 Years Ago! Ha! Ha! Ha! How do we fall down to salute
with peals of Heh heh hehhh! That the Beats created change
without a drop of blood!

In 1965 it was all we could do to force-cajole the writers
for *Time* magazine not to reinforce the spurious Anslinger
synapse, that pot puff leads to the poppy fields—
but now the states are setting hemp free! Ten years of
coded foment! Heh! Heh! Heh!

Yesterday: the freeing of verse

Today: pot

Tomorrow: free food in the supermarket

Heh! heh! heh!

And finally let us ne'r forget that this is the Age of Ha Ha Hee!
    Ha Ha Hee is such a valuable tool
    in the tides of social transformation!

    Ha Ha Hee will set you free from worm-farm angst
    Ha Ha Hee will even curdle the fires of jealousy!

    Ha Ha Hee outvotes the Warrior Caste
    Ha Ha Hee doth whelm the self-devouring quarrel

    Ha Ha Hee peals out through all the cosmos
            mandorla'd with

        poet angels holding Plato's
            7 single syllables
                in a tighter harmony than the
                    early Beach boys—

    This is the poets' era
    and we shall all walk
    crinkle-toed upon the smooth
    cold thrill of Botticelli's shell.

                    —Written for
                    the New Year's
                    Reading at
                    St. Mark's Church
                    January 1, 1975

# And the Generals with Wolf Masks

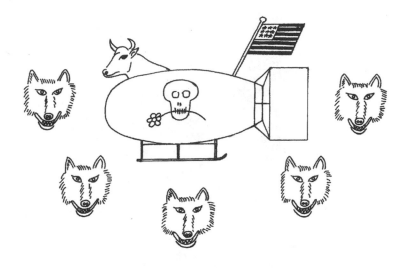

And the generals
with wolf masks

crowded about
the bomb

to seize it from those
who had made it

and Hathor
was angry

—1976

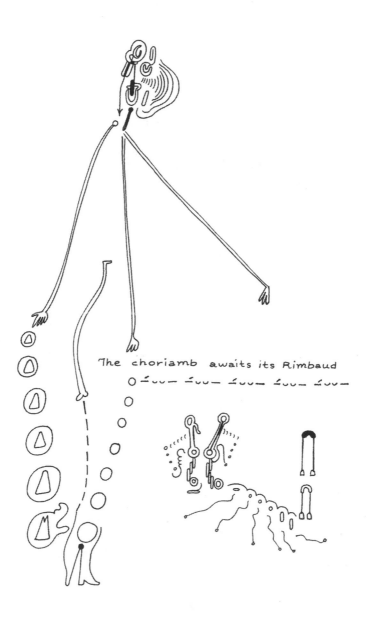

The choriamb awaits its Rimbaud

## Why Hesitate to Know All Gentle Things?

Why hesitate
to know all gentle things?
And then, this:
to feel again your "skin-fins"
as you have determined it.

to make Law
of our amours,
free again.

To read again

of thee and thine.

Across the
purloined space

To crochet
our desires
into the silver stomach
of the numinal
tundra.

Yazzah!

<u>Yes:</u>  once again,

yes,              yes,              yes.

## Sappho's Poem Beginning Φαινεται μοι

Equal to the gods
is the man who sits
in front of you leaning closely
and hears you sweetly speaking
and the lust-licking laughter
of your mouth, oh it makes my
heart beat in flutters!

When I look at you
Brochea, not a part of my
voice comes out,
but my tongue breaks,
and right away
a delicate fire runs just beneath
my skin,

I see a dizzy nothing,
my ears ring with noise,
the sweat runs down
upon me, and a trembling
that I cannot stop
seizes me limb and loin,
o I am greener than grass, and
death seems so near . . .

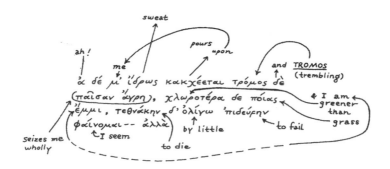

## Sappho's Hymn to Aphrodite

Splendor-throned, deathless
love-ploy-plotting Aphrodite,
Daughter of Zeus, I pray to thee.
Do not overwhelm my heart
with cares and griefs, my Queen.

But, come to me now, if ever now and
again in the past, listening from afar,
you heard my prayers, and harnessed
your golden chariot to leave
your father's realm, thy chariot
drawn by two swift swans with
thickly flashing wings from heaven
through the middle of the upper sky
down upon the darkling earth.

The swift swans brought thee
quickly near, o Aphrodite,
and you asked me,
with a smile on your deathless face,
what it was that
made me suffer so, and why
was I crying out, what
did I want most specially
to assuage my raging heart?

"Whom shall I persuade,"
you asked, "to bring you
the treasure of torrid love?
Who, o Sappho,
who wrongs thee?

If she flees thee
swiftly shall
she dance at
thy heels

If she does not
take thy gifts
swiftly shall she
give

If she loves thee not,
swiftly shall
she glide in
the beams of desire,
even be she unwilling
at first," you said
to me Aphrodite.

O come to me at once, o
Aphrodite, and free me
from this harsh love pain!

That which my soul  craves to be done
do it!  o do it!
You yourself, in living person
be thou my ally!

# Arrows of Translation

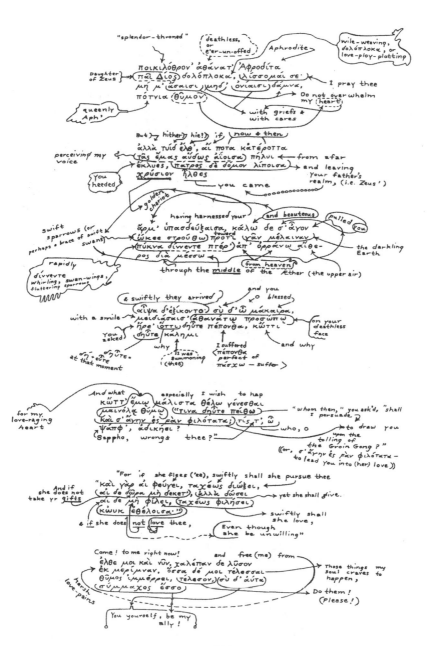

# The Cutting Prow

He couldn't paint, he couldn't sculpt. He was confined to a
wheelchair, and gripped with *timor mortis*. From his bed at
night he'd draw on the ceiling with a long stick with crayon
attached. Yet somehow he adjusted his creativity, finding a new
mix of the muses, so that from the spring of 1952 through the
spring of '53, in his final creative months, Henri Matisse was
able to produce some of the finest art of the century—works
such as *The Swimming Pool, Large Decoration with Masks, The
Negress, Memory of Oceania, Women and Monkeys*, and the
smaller *Blue Nude* series. He thought he could scissor the
essence of a thing, its "sign" as he termed it, as if he had vision
in Plato's world of Forms.

> The genius was 81
> Fearful of blindness
> Caught in a wheelchair
> Staring at death
>
> But the Angel of Mercy
> gave him a year
> to scissor some shapes
> to soothe the scythe
>
> and shriek!    shriek!
>            became
>      swawk!    swawk!
>        the peace of
>          scissors.
>
> There was something besides
> the inexpressible
>            <u>thrill</u>
> of cutting a beautiful shape—
>
> for
> Each thing had a "sign"

Each thing had a "symbol"
Each thing had a cutting form
      —swawk  swawk—

to scissor seize.

"One must study an object a long time,"
  the genius said,
"to know what its sign is."

The scissors were his scepter
The cutting
was as the prow of a barque
to sail him away.

There's a photograph
        which shows him
sitting in his wheelchair
bare foot touching the floor
drawing with criss-cross steel
a shape in the gouache

His helper sits near him
till he hands her the form
to pin to the wall

He points with a stick
how he wants it adjusted
This way and that,
            minutitudinous.

The last blue iris blooms at
the top of its stalk

      scissors/scepter
      cutting/prow

      (sung)

Keep those scissors flashing in the
World of Forms, Henri Matisse

The cutting of the scissors
was the prow of a boat
          to sail him away
The last blue iris
        blooms at the top
              on a warm spring day

Ah, keep those scissors flashing in the
World of Forms, Henry Matisse

Sitting in a wheelchair
bare foot touching the floor
Angel of Mercy
          pushed him over
                next to Plato's door

Scissor  scepter  cutting prow
Scissor  scepter  cutting prow
Scissor  scepter  cutting prow
Scissor  scepter  cutting prow

          ahh
      swawk  swawk

            ahh
        swawk  swawk

            ahh
        swawk  swawk

—1981

# Hymn to O

There was a term
        of Anaximander's
inflamed my youth

τὸ ἄπειρον

    to apeiron
    The Uncrossable
    The Boundless

& really, for years, went batty
      for  to apeiron

τὸ ἄπειρον

used to think
all the time about the Apeiron

*Peace Eye,* my book of verse, was part of it
Eye-Heart-Minds
        shooting the rapids
          to vanish in the Lake
            outbound to Peace Eye
that was part. To make
poems history again—that
was the sum.

Anaximander graphed the thrill of the first map, the
"perimetros," as they called it.

I had a vision
after Olson's death
of two different things

One that he walked up
to a twisted circle of rope
with the ends lashed together

where they met—

The shen-sign of Egypt
sigil Aeternitatis

and leaped through it
as if it were a tire swing

the second, that somewhere somehow
when that famous ferry's pole struck
the brass shores

he ran into a posse of
pre-Socratics

who drew him
that is to say, forthwith!

into a delicate discourse

There can never
be enough of dignity
when bards
fly flash
to the
shore.

I can feel you Charles
when I stare at the froth
of Gloucester's tanny rocks

You're there, next to the O-Boat,
talking with Alfred Whitehead

Anaximander is there
holding a
10-dimensional sphere

A lone Ionian column
stands on a hill
I see you O
bending at the base
writing a line upon the whiteness

You dive, again again
like a dolphin on ancient silver
through the shen-sign's ring.

Anaximander
with a perimetros
of "Earth & the Sea
     & the Sphere of the Sky"
and the endless oatmeal
of the Apeiron

Hey Charlie O Charlie
Olson has entered
the cartouche

        and this is a prayer
        that he and Anaximander
        walk down through the fields together

        o what a map they will make

## The Ice

*—a true tale*

It was New Year's
eve 1958 and there was
no place to make love

They were sitting in the Figaro Café
at MacDougal & Bleecker Streets
sipping an orzata and a grenadine

Bought a small bottle of brandy
went to
Fort Tryon Park
Washington Heights
Columbia Boat Basin

climbed high up in the
rocks        there had been snow

making love
                    steep incline between rocks
            tennis shoes gripping
opened his coat and they
wiggled off the rock
and slid down the ice-flow

"We're sliding."   They couldn't stop
                        & the ice thrilled her buttocks
                            for maybe 5 or 6 feet
                        down the twiggy glaciation

# Ramamir

*—a tune for the Pulse Lyre*

It was the fall of
'58 when
we met in Greek class
at N.Y.U.

She was there
because of an interest
in archaeology

& I that my mother had
said that a gentleman
reads Greek and Latin

(plus, who could scan
Pound's *Cantos* without them?)

She was 17; she'd been
the valedictorian
of her class
at the Yeshiva; and
when we waited by
the elevator after class
she had the habit
of twirling one whole turn
in her long red
Chesterfield coat
with a belt
and two big white buttons
in the back.

One afternoon
as we walked across
Washington Square
past the large gray circle

of the fountain
I said, "I guess
we'll have to join
the Beat Generation."

"What's that?" she asked.

It was just about then
I gave her the nickname
Ramamir

We used to hang out
in dusty bookstores
and in coffee shops
to hear the poets read

She wore those stylish
spear-toed high heels
or Alan Block
high-lace sandals

She wore black kohl
around her eyes
and a leather vest
laced up the sides

Her black wool turtleneck
held heaven's heaviness
She was my blond-haired
diamond sutra

And when we made love
by the Central Park Zoo
ahh the gods above
they watched us loving

And the police man
standing on the bridge too
He watched us loving
by the Central Park Zoo

It was so intense
we soon forgot
the detectives her father
hired to follow
us around
because I wasn't Jewish

I wrote poems about her
and shyly showed them
over Café Viennese
at the Figaro

with lines like
"She was the night
and the moon through her eyes

was as white
           as the drapes of a
       marble statue"

              or

"Ramamir grabbed the long moon
in her teeth and dashed home
to devour in her den"

              and other lunalalic
                     phantasms
       beaming from Ramamir's eyes

For seasons
her home was hell
as her parents
tried to stomp us down

And sometimes it seemed
as if demons
were driving bonkers-stanchions
to cage us apart

Ahh Ramamir Ramamir
my kohl-eyed rebel girl
somehow we persevered

and now we make maple syrup
on Mead's Mountain Road,
sap-spiles dripping in praise
of the force
that brought us together.

## My Boat Was Overturned

My boat was overturned
It was hard
to set it right

when part of me
loved the waterfall
and part the land


At 5 a.m.
I sat on the bed
with my face bent forward
into my hands

wondering how
to get out the door
to you

## You Were the One I Loved

You were the one I loved
watching the solar barge
on Tenth street

We stood to gaze at the heavens
to watch for the sun boat's oar
over Tenth street

oh it's wrong to speak   of freedom   and peace
unless   your love    is justly done

I could weep I could moan forever
for the wrongs that I have done
on Tenth street

but there's no turning back the time-stream
to be a better man

You picked the wildflowers darling
and pressed them in a poetry book
              (for your dirty bard)

Tenth street is burnt and gone
but you and I still love as one
and the Eye of Peace stares on

# Wounded Water

*—and what's the Work?*
*To ease the pain of living,*
*Everything else, drunken*
*dumbshow*

*—Allen Ginsberg*
*"Memory Gardens"*

I have swum for twenty years
in the creeks of Wounded Water
and the tears that I have shed
are swallowed up in Wounded Water

All the faces     of those who've gone to harm
reflect around our faces
staring 'bove the roil
            of Wounded Water

Swaying in the water, amidst the lily leaves
tangles of telephone wires
and smashed guts of tape recorders
waving and weaving and swaying
in the glut of Wounded Water

O, the files!  once so full of data-gnarls
lie chaotic as a marble's marls
and folders of sleaze     blow in the breeze
and the pages plop     to float then drop
beneath the brink     of Wounded Water

The oceans of grief slosh by slosh by
the pylons of anger and harm—
We may hope to defy and disarm it
or snatch another from the fire,
just before we drown
in the gully of Wounded Water

Ease th' pain! Ease th' pain!
and stand, with art, that elegant plier
in the torrent, rising higher,
of moiling, roiling Wounded Water

# In di Gasn, tsu di Masn

*(Into the Streets, to the Masses)*

## Yiddish Speaking Socialists
## of the Lower East Side

*—a history written to be chanted and sung,*
*accompanied by the Pulse Lyre*


They came when the Czar banned the Yiddish
                              theater in 1882
They came when the iron-tipped Cossack's whip
                    flicked in the face of their mother
They came when their parents were cheated out of
                              their farms in Vilna
They came to escape the peasants at Easter, hacking
                              with scythes and knives
They came when the Revolution of 1905 was crushed
They came when the soldiers broke up their socialist
                              presses in Crakow
They fled from Siberia, dungeons and work camps,
                    for printing leaflets and fliers—


        pamphlets and poems and leaflets and fliers
        to spread in the workshops
        spread in the streets
        spread in the factories

        in the spirit the era had spawned
        the spirit the era had spawned


            "*In di gasn*
                  *tsu di masn*
            Into the streets
                  to the masses"


They came to Antwerp and then to London
                    and then to Ludlow Street

to make a New World
inside a New World
at century's turn—
The Yiddish speaking socialists
of the Lower East Side

Some remembered
        with pangs and tears
                the beautiful rural life
                        wrested away


Mushroom hunting in the dampened woods
Bundles of grain in the carts
Market day in the shtetl

Some strained their eyes
for the gold-paved streets of the West
just to be greeted by one of those
"incomprehensible economic collapses"
that New York gives to its poor

The East Side
        had been slums
                since the overcrowdings
                        after the War of 1812—

but the tenement rents of 1903
                were higher than
                        nearby "better" places

2/3's of them owned by speculators
getting 15 to 30% (or more)

so that a family of ten
                was jammed
                        in a two-room flat

plus boarders!

and a leafleteer
            in desperation
                        lay aside his ink
to open a curbside store
            with a gutter plank
                        and 3 brown bales of rag

Or they carried the cribs
            to the hallway
                        to set up a sweatshop—

They were not alone

from thousands of windows
            came the clackety-clacks
                        of foot-treadled sewing machines

and the drum-like sounds
            of long bladed scissors
                        chewing on oaken boards

and the lungs turned gray
                        with tidbits of tweed
and the red hot irons
on the tops of the coal stoves
to smooth out the bundles of cloth

and the sweet gulps of air
                        on Cherry Street
walking out kinks of the legs at dusk
from a day at the torturing treadle.

A rose curled around the mallet of pov.
The Lower East Side
was the strongest socialist zone
                        in the United States
for the first twenty years
of this century.

It was a
        wild world of words
and everywhere
        the song
            of the wild lecture
arose above a wild lectern—

Scott Nearing
        at the Rand School of Social Science
Morris Hillquit
        at the Workmen's Circle
Emma Goldman
        at the Educational Alliance
Eugene Debs
        coming in from Terra Haute
                to Webster Hall

And political discussions
        on the summertime roofs
            in Yiddish, Russian, Polish, & English—

wild world of words

Labor Day parades from East Broadway
to Union Square
Cousins on the floor
        from fleeing Siberia
            after the Revolution of 1905

Union meetings at the Labor Lyceum on E. 4th—
        Flashes of the Ideal
            in murk
                in muck
                    in mire

Talking all night at the Café Royale
                at 12th and 2nd Avenue

        after the Yiddish plays at
        the Kessler or Tomashevski Theaters

Garment worker rallies at Cooper Union
Joining the Women's Trade Union League
Fighting for a shorter work week
6 and 1/2 days to six, and then
to 44 hours, on the way to 40

Flashes of the Ideal
in murk
in muck
in mire

*In di gasn*
*tsu di masn*

To make a New World
inside the New World
at Century's turn
the Yiddish speaking socialists
of the Lower East Side.

For twenty years they grew.
They filled the arenas
and packed the streets

though those who stand
in the bowl of shrieks
know how the bowl
stands silent
so often
when the votes are
counted.

But there was a party in the streets
The Lower East Side had never seen
the night in 1914 that Meyer London,
whose father had worked in an anarchist print shop,
was elected to Congress

They danced and sang
through Rutgers Square past the *Daily Forward*

till the sun blushed the color of communes
above the docks.

Meyer London served for three terms
until the democrats and republicans in
the State Assembly
gerrymandered his district.

In 1917 the Socialist Party of NYC
sent ten assemblymen to Albany
and seven to the NYC board of aldermen
and even elected a municipal judge

while Morris Hillquit
pulled 22% of the vote for mayor—

It looked   like a Socialist surge
might move    as a spill of thrills
out through the state

> *In di gasn*
> *tsu di masn*

to make a New World
inside the New World
            at century's turn
the Yiddish Speaking Socialists
                of the Lower East Side

And then, in the spring of 1917
                the U.S. Congress
                        voted for war

The Socialists
        met in St. Louis
                that same April

& issued
        what was known as
                the St. Louis Resolution—

"We call upon the
                    workers of all countries
        to refuse support
                    to their governments
                                in their wars."

Some were sympathetic
                    to the strong socialist and
                                union movements in Germany

in a struggle
            against
                    Czarist barbarism—

others felt it
            was just a distracting disturbance
                                between Russian
                                    & German militaries.

The Lower East Side was split.
            The pressure to support
                        their new country

was great—not that pogroms
            by the Brooklyn Bridge were feared
                    though the dirk-tined rioting peasant's rake
                                was not that far
                                            in the past.

The Wilson administration
                    generated war hysteria
Scott Nearing, Eugene Debs
                        went to jail
the government threatened
the mailing rights of the *Jewish Daily Forward*
and other socialist papers
opposing the war.

And then it
was different

after the war.

There was hideous inflation
and F.O.B.
       Fear of Bolsheviks—

and many, mayhemic forces
were set against the
Lower East Side socialist zone.

The anti-red hysteria was nationwide
The Wobblies were crushed
The strikers of Seattle crushed
The Palmer Raids
Federal troops used to club down
                    honest dispute
Emma Goldman deported
Five socialists expelled from the
               NY Legislature
and the socialist Victor Berger
banned from his seat in the Congress.

There was a split in
the Socialist Party in 1919

& the birth of the Communist Party.

You think there was factionalism
in the 1960s, say—
The factions of 1920 hissed
like 35,000 ganders
          in an amanita valley—

and a democratic socialist
in the '20s and '30s
was wedged in pain among
the sharp-tongued Moscow leftists
and sharp-tongued bitter-shitter rightists.

Oh they failed
to spread the East Side zone
into a broader country
of psychopathic landboomers
& smug townies
who thought they could hog
the keys to the sky

There was the fact that
a climate of lectures and rallies
can aid in the first rough forward step,
                              but rarely the second—

They knew with all the hurt of their years
how the socialist fervor fell—
and the failure of those
                    who had seen the socialist dawn
to break it from sea to sea.


Most of them fled the rubbly slums,
and tens of thousands more,
for few there are
who joy
to live in dirt

They joked how the ships
brought the greenhorns to Rutgers Square
as the moving vans
took the radicals to the Bronx.

            For most
            the game
            was to get OUT

            but for some
            like Congressman London
            the East Side
            was the
                        world

in which to stay

He was there all his life
till killed by a car
as he crossed 2nd Avenue—

Shelley had Keats in his pocket
London had Chekhov

Oh they failed
but I can hear their ghosts
walk down the cobbles
outside the St. Mark's Church

the poets, the strikers, the printers,
the firebrands, the leafleteers—
comrades when the word had its glow—

with a passion for Justice
                that never fades away
though heartbreak
                to know
                        that they had failed

to make a New World
inside the New World
at century's turn
They were the Yiddish speaking socialists
of the Lower East Side.

••••••

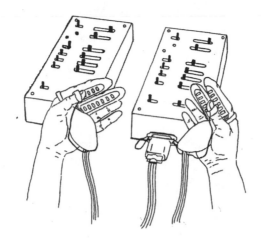

**Drawing of Pulse Lyre by Miriam Sanders**

Note from author: in researching this poem, the books below supplied much useful and thrilling information:

*The House on Henry Street,* Lillian Wald
*Memoirs of a Revolutionary,* Eva Broido
*World of Our Fathers,* Irving Howe
*How the Other Half Lives,* Jacob Riis
*Labor and Farmer Parties in the United States,* Nathan Fine
*Born One Year Before the 20th Century,* Minnie Fisher

## Advice from St. Augustine

*—from* The Z/D Generation

Eleutherarchy has taken to the airwaves
since the days of Dostoevsky,
and the Freedom is there for all

Therefore, NEVER HESITATE TO OPEN
    UP A CASE FILE

        EVEN UPON THE BLOODIEST
            OF BEASTS OR PLOTS!

We will see the day of

    RELENTLESS
    PURSUIT OF DATA!

    Interrogate the Abyss!

To go after an item of time,
    (as Olson says, p. 134 of
    *The Human Universe & Other Essays,*

    the essence is to
"KNOW THE NEW FACTS EARLY.")

        Draw a graph or glyph
        of your investigation target

surround the glyph
with gnosis-vectors

pointing to the target

and never surrender!


Learn everything to be known
about your
data-target

then proceed with Question Lists   (very important
                                                              to have precise
                                                              written, Q-Lists)


toward the

data-target
$\triangle$
dt


Then it's robot-targeting:

if you get knocked down,
                    flame-mouthed, confused by the target's
                    hype or threats,

stand up, reassemble your Q-Lists,
and proceed again toward the data-target

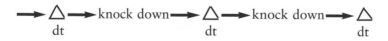

$$\longrightarrow \underset{dt}{\triangle} \longrightarrow \text{knock down} \longrightarrow \underset{dt}{\triangle} \longrightarrow \text{knock down} \longrightarrow \underset{dt}{\triangle}$$

Holding ever in mind
The Three Adverbs

$$\boxed{\text{C/R/E}}$$

Ceaselessly/Relentlessly/Ethically.

Not that there will be no danger, though we urge the
Three Adverbs upon you
Just keep in mind, when you advance
upon your $\dfrac{\triangle}{dt}$

St. Augustine's dictum,
very suitable to remember,
stress-questioning hostile data-sources:

"The wicked persecute
the good w/ the blindness
of the passion that animates them,
while the good pursue the
wicked with a wise discretion."

## The Art of the Elegant Footnote

The art of the elegant
footnote is ever to
be practiced

    (a pig farm mentioned
    in the *Maximus Poems* is
    no longer there—so, the
    elegant footnote describes
    the pig farm from the minds
    of those who remember)

A footnote is like a dangling data-cluster
much like a shaped piece of metal in
a Calder mobile

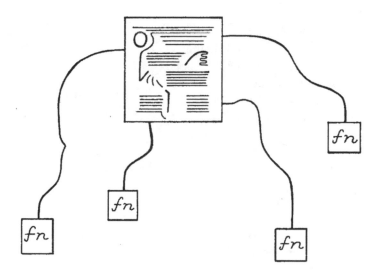

## Hymn to Maple Syrup

The leaves from
the wet, black sugar maples
hang down in the icy fog—
just a few
the color of blanched-out butterscotch,

above the weed-spiked snow.

& the pine tree's bough
springs up from the snow bank
where it was jammed for months
and nods up and down,
spraying the air about
with a fine shaking
of icy granules.

The sheet of ice across the creek
is cracked here and there.
The creek depth had dropped
since midwinter rains
and an eery foot-high gap is left
'tween ice and icy flow.
You can see it in the breach
where the deer drink
and the blue jays hop for a dangerous sip

Soon giant tiles of it
will begin to drop
from the ice-floor
down upon the blue stone roil

and it's time to boil.

My pockets are cold with short metal tubes called
spiles

with a knob-like protuberance
on upper edge
to keep the sap bags
from falling off.

I feel affection for the
rough swirls of ancient maple bark
for each giant sugar
        is a Patting Tree

and sometimes I stop
to hug a maple as huge
as two people reaching
around it,
sliding my arms past
spile scars of seasons past,
dark circles
        in dark crusts
the winter mittens touch,

and then to lean
with brace & bit
the knob of it
        pressing the chest,
and chew through
the gray to the butter-tan wood.

The wood-curls at the hole's mouth
turn moist
as soon as I screw
out the drill bit

Then gently to tap
the spile in the hole
& the sap runs shiny
out of the shiny tip

while sliding the sap bag
upside down

then twisting it
straight so it's hooked
on the spile.

Some trees are big enough
for more than one
and sometimes I worry that plastic bags
will tinge the sap with pollution

Across the creek
is an open front sapping shed
with an old Norge stove
once gas, but now
outfitted for wood

I've draped it overwinter
with a plastic sheet
to ward away rust.

Time now to rake the leaves away
& set up the stovepipe flue
(stored in the garage)
which curves from the stove and up
then angles at 90 degrees through the wall
then up again to a
tin-hatted hood by the roof

Inside the Norge
are two lines of concrete
laid front to back
and topped with a

row of grills
that look like Hibachi grates

I lift them away
and shovel the ashes
of last year's final fire
from the trough beneath

Most of the shed is saved
for a gnarly stack
of branches and boards
much of it wind-fall
& some from the Woodstock dump

the game is to make the
syrup for free.

Today I raid
the neighbor's woods for
fallen birch

skwonching through snow
to drag a tall white log
in a hesitant lurch
across the blue stone property wall
pennants of loosened bark
flip-flapping white on white

& the long end leaving
a deep dug furrow
like a giant possum's trail

down to the Norge's mouth
to be chainsawed.

The correct beatnik hour
for emptying the sap bags
is 2 a.m.

Back & forth th' galoshes skwonch

scaring the deer
from the yew-berry bush

I rotate the bag on its spile
and pour the sap in a metal pail
then walk through the dark
to the 40-gallon holding can
by the shed

steady steady
dodging the low-hanging white pine's
bough as the raspberry wands
and the China rose whack the legs

trying to keep the sap from sloshing
with little frothy waves
to douse the knuckles and gloves
as cold as the ocean at Gloucester.

It's a fine aerobic sapper's trudge
a fourth of a mile or more
tree to can to tree to can
till all of the
bags hang
flaccid again.

There's a long rectangular pan
with handles on the ends
for the stove top
from the Kingston China & Bar Supply

I pour a few gallons
to fill it.

It takes so long to
build a fire!
as if the gnarl-pile's kindling
were haunted
by a water-haint.

I want it now!
Flames! Forthwithity!

I love to boil at night,
beneath the sap shed's single bulb
from the ceiling,
keeping the Norge's door wide open
and stuffed with overlength wood.
The first rush is sweetest and best
they say
and so it is tonight
as the room width fills
with billows of paradise steam.

Tending the boil I sit
out there on
an old oak school desk-chair

working on poems or tales
to bulb light and Norge light
like jotting notes
by the forge of Hephaestus

pausing to flick the
shiny skuz
that roils to the top of the pan
to a corner
with a slotted spoon

learning to love the sp-u-lapp of it
sp-u-lapping the barren floor.

Or you can put on a fresh tray
then go to the house
              to type a few poems
but you have to be careful
to return in a hurry
to add more logs
and flick the skuz

Tarry too long
        over *Star Trek*
and you'll lose the sap
in a caramel ooze

It's sad to have to hurl
a hissing tray of sap-gravy
down into the creek, kneeling
to scrape long scabs of carbonated black
from its sides.

It takes about
an hour
to boil away a pan

You learn how to tell
how close it is
dipping a spoon for a taste

or you know how low it must be
to be nearly done.

The mittens & potholders
reach for the handles
and turn

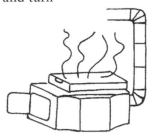

the tray to the side for a better grip,
quickly,
for the flame-tips rise
through slits in the stove top
singe-ing the hair on the wrist
'tween glove & sleeve,

The steam so fierce
it sears the eyes
so I close them, turning slowly
determined not to slosh syrup
onto the floor, or worse,
and walk four steps in blindness to
a table in back
where I tilt the tray so the sap pours out
of a corner
                down to a metal pot.
For a second I open my eyes to
sight in for the pour

and then the "spoawwt!"-sound
of sudden syrup
                on chilly steel.

I set the tray-pan back on the fire
then rush to dip fresh sap from
the can

before the tray doth burn.

I boil up another batch
then pour it too in the pot
till it brims

and I carry it over the bridge
to the house
bring back another pot
till it brims
and on and on
till I quit at the dawn.

You have to be careful
stunned at sun-up
walking with the final boil
toward the creek
eye brims red
                from facing the steam
not to trip on the mulberry stump

or slide in the slosh
of the rail-less bridge
with blobs of 210 fahrenheit syrup
sizzling your tissue.

Back in the house
it's the peace of zzzzz's,
the smell of maple
             in moustache & hair
& reddened wrists from the sap sun.

The next morning Miriam & I
finish it off in the kitchen
half gallon by half gallon
heating it up to a boil
then checking the temperature.

(First you see where water boils.
It varies according to pressure.
Most days it's 209.5 or 210, but
some it's 211 or 12.  And then
we add another seven degrees,
for our height above the sea,
and that's the maple syrup point)

We use a dial thermometer

clipped to the pan edge.
Sometimes the eyes get again
a hint of the pain of a
lobster's eyes
leaning too close to read
the sugar-crusted dial.

Then one of us holds

a hammock-shaped padding
                    of cheese cloth
hand to hand
while the other pours the
syrup through it
into the jars to be sealed.

Some years the
sap keeps coming & coming & coming!

a never-ceasing flood
                    to be boiled
and I feel guilty
if I let any spoil
till finally I yell,
            "No! No more!"
and pull the bags from the trees
and pry off the spiles
with a hammer's claw
& twig up the holes.

And then it's done
for a year.


        CODA


There's nothing to it.
It's like the ocean
or raked Zen sand.
It's empty.  Yet full
of the best.

It helps you to set
aside the fear
of lumps in the skin,

to save all that was
and toss all that will
in the sweet roil of foam
in a tray on the hill.

## The Plane

The plane
flies over
the lakes
in the pine barrens

& the moon
gleams
suddenly
on each

like a quick
flash—

it's startling.

  the 3-quarter
moon
up there like
a mail sack
full of pleasure

pond 'pon pond

till it stops
& I feel

a longing
to see more

pondic
lun' flash!

more!  more!

     —Flying from Albany
     to Albany
     October 5, 1984

## Consolatio Naturae

*—for Gary Snyder*

When I showed Gary some entries from my diary
mostly observations of outdoor scenes
during an environmental conference
he said I should read them that night
during our public reading, and so thereafter
I considered them poems.

1.

The oak tree
flowers, tiny,
looking under the
ten power lens
like clusters
of unripe bananas

2.

The chickadee
biting & shaking
          the cluster
                of maple seeds

like six tiny
mountain maracas

3.

The deep
      liquid
            bap-at-ta-bap-at-ta

in perfect time
          of the rosy headed
              woodpecker

high on the thick
          shagbark
like a clavé player
      with a complicated fill
            in a Perez Prado gig

          in 1948

4.

Deer
   front yard
      rose petal
         forehead
           rain

5.

The woodpecker nestlings
have shove-spilled
      out of their
      birthplace
      high in the old
      acid rain damaged ash

and play together
on the limbs nearby

like children
in a schoolyard

6.

The wind
struck
the azalea flower
and the black-winged butterfly
licking nectar
clung flutteringly thereon
as the bow dipped down


7.

The Career

The full moon seems to poise
on the icy branch
then disappears


8.

The clump of thin-stem'd tree flowers
lies dried on this page
where they had fallen
yesterday morning

I kiss them with my pen
as they melt upon the
                 Great Tongue

9.

*Probably as Important*
*as Finishing that Poem*

Prop up with stones
the young sugar maple
in danger of
        being rained down into the creek

—whose roots cling
to the bank
shouting "I want to live!"


10.


I lick the lichen
on the
        tall skinny Black Oak

It does not taste
like Wheaties

In fact there's
            no word yet
for lichen-taste


11.

The old hippie encampment
not much more than a few tires now
& some broken tepee poles
& a milk crate
        stuffed with goneness

12.

The rule is
to drive slow
         enough
on country roads
to avoid
smashing into
swallowtails


13.

The splotch
     of hawk scat
like the fling
     of a 1950 Action Painter

on the stone of the walkway

may explain
what happened
     to my chipmunk


14.

The St. John's bread
trampled
     to shoe-shards
outside the liquor store
because people have
forgotten it's a
     delicacy

15.

The sugar maple fell
in the winter howl

I cringe as I chainsaw
it's so green & juicy
                    still alive

that I can't
            keep cutting

something that so much
wants to be standing tall again


                                16.

                        In the
                        100 years
                        of warming

                        the birch grove
                        hobbles
                        across Route 28
                        & up the valley

                        toward the
                                    Arctic Circle

17.

She didn't
want to go
to Albany

"I want to
stay home
& water
the white
snake root,
& the
wild flowers"


18.

I'm feeling
        food chain fatigue
as the wet baby jay
hangs from the
                crow

19.

I didn't like the sound

of the raccoon
attacking the squirrel nest
up in the white pine

so I backed our car around
honking & shouting, "Hey! Get out of here!"
& flashing the lights

so that it walked
back down face first
& galumphed toward the road


20.

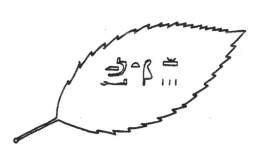

The feather of justice
rests on the Leaf

# Circles of Ice

*—for Tom Bryan, sap man extraordinaire*

The woolly white dog named Roshi
lay
    on the gray snow bank
by the flappy-barked yellow birch
        next to the sap house

as we trudged into the forest
to empty the buckets.

In each a chilly discus of sap ice
floats
to be flung away
        as we pour.
Most fall down with a crackly thud
and flick flecks of sap on our boots
but a few land on their edges
and roll down the hill.

Sometimes that's
        what life seems like—
circles of ice
rolling down a hill

but not today,
for you can lean at the edge
of the freshly emptied sugarbush
and listen
        to the perf-sap

that is, to the subtle sounds
of sap-drips
        plinking the pails.

Tom has an idea for a musical instrument—
You record the various drips
and put them on chips

"a Sap Lyre"

The Tambourine for the hay field
The Panpipes for the vineyard
The Sap Lyre for the sugarbush.

Back in the sugar house
we wadded *The New York Times*
and tossed it into the metal mouth
of the Small Brothers boiler

"Reagan Kills Farm Aid" was
the head of the first page aflame.

It wasn't many minutes of hurling
the six-foot slabs in the firebox
till Tom Bryan was pouring
the first few gallons
through filtering funnels of cloth

and woolly Roshi waited
with the eagerness
of 20,000,000 years
for Tom to pour her a
taste in a jar lid

and the circles of ice
roll down the hill.

—April 1985

# Hymn to Archilochus

*—for Joe Cardarelli*

On the rocky isle of Paros*
    2,700 years ago
        was born a bard
who smote the strings of his lyre
        with a newness
          that made them gasp
            for a 1,000 years

His name was Archilochus
He was thought by the ancients
        the equal of Homer
The halves of his brain
      shared secrets by the billion
          to make it new.

From Plutarch**
we learn that Archilochus
made many inventions:

the ithyphallic trochaic trimeter
the recitative
    (rhythmical recitation
        of poetry to the lyre or flute)
the combination of unlike measures
the epode
    (long line followed by short)
the tetrameter
the cretic
the prosodiac
the combination of epibatic paeon with the iambic
the lengthened "heroic" with prosodiac and cretic

 * one of the Cyclades Islands southeast of Athens
** *On Music*

the combination of singing and recitation
within the same poem
and he was the first to tune his lyre
an octave higher than his voice

He wrote the
victory song
at the Olympics

In later centuries
they used to
stitch together
a rhapsody
of his poems & songs
& tour the islands
doing
A Night of Archilochus

He was the first great confessional poet
They spoke of his raging iambics
He was engaged to a woman named Neobule
but her father intervened
and prevented it
and he wrote about him
with such a bitter pulse
that the verses
were said to cause a suicide

Critics accused Archilochus of
"slandering himself"
because, through his poesy,
people down through the centuries
knew he was the son of a slave woman, Enipo,
that pov drove him from Paros to Thasos*
that he was adulterous & lecherous.

He was the first of the poets
to de-macho his art

Once he let them strip away his shield
on the field of battle

* Island off the coast of Thrace

and laughed of it later in trochees & dactyls*

an act that got him thrown
                out of Sparta—
                        The South Africa
                                of 600 B.C.

What an honor
                when the Spartan secret police
ordered his books removed
for erotolalia.

He was a mercenary
                as well as a bard
He must have looked like a samurai
                standing on the marble chips
                                of Paros
                with greaves on the legs
        & a horschair plume on his helmet

his tortoise shell lyre packed away
                                with his poems
                in a sheepskin satchel.

    O bards
            ponder Archilochus
                    you who think
                        "Hey, my poems are going to last
                        all the way till the Milky Way
                        explodes."

    Your archives
            bulging in acid-free binders
                        at UC-San Diego
    and a staff
            of graduate students
                    sorting them clean!

* Ἀσπίδι μὲν Σαΐων τις ἀγάλλεται, ἣν παρὰ θάμνῳ
    ἔντος, ἀμώμητον κάλλιπον οὐκ ἐθέλων,
  αὐτὸν δ᾽ ἐκ μ᾽ ἐσάωσα τί μοι μέλει ἀσπὶς ἐκείνη;
    ἐρρέτω· ἐξαῦτις κτήσομαι οὐ κακίω

The fireman felt the wall
                above my bed
just where I'd taped
                a quote from a poem
                                by Robert Kelly.

On the blanket were all of the books
of Charles Olson
and my notes for
                the Olson Memorial Lectures

when I was
                wounded by fire in
                        the frothsome night

"Why are you saving those books?"
                        the fireman asked
pointing his axe
                toward the stereo
hosing down my wall of verse
and chopping the plaster.

As I scooped up the books
I thought of Archilochus
whose work comes down to us
                    in pitiful tatters

gone
      shredded
            stomped
                abyssed

gone with the fires
            that burned Alexandria
gone with the disrepute
                and disrespect
gone with the book-burning frenzy
            of Christians and Moslems
gone with the mold spores
            alighting atop the

long chains of molecules
        holding the structure of paper

for a 1,000-year lunch
        of the lines of Archilochus

The first large magnetic body
that passes too close to earth
will erase the tapes
The one that crashes
        will burn the books

and the sky shall spit
        your poems out
            like pellets of fire

The home town of Catullus
        was Verona
where they saved a single manuscript
but no one saved Archilochus.

Your wounded verses sing
across the ages
        o Archilochus
I can see you standing
        on a hillside
holding your 4-string lyre
and how you were an inventer!
striking the twisted strings
on the palmwood sounding board
        with a limberlimbic meter
            whose waves
                slosh gently
and faintly
all the way to my burning wall,

and it was you who said

εἰ γὰρ ὣς ἐμοὶ γένοιτο χεῖρα Νεοβούλης θιγεῖν

"If only it could happen
                 that I could touch
                           the hand of Neobule"

          (sung)

There used to be a poet named Archilochus
one of the greatest of them all
Oh there's nothing of his poetry now
except some scattered lines

I wish we could hear Archilochus
play his four-stringed lyre
Oh to hear some great poetry
to make the world entire

Oh I learned from Archilochus
about the Nightingale
Oh I long to hold the nightingale
nesting in my hands

and I love to spend the Catskill spring
the Catskill spring with you
but you know that there's a hunger there
to touch the nightingale

Oh they talk so elegantly
about eternity
Oh I sing to you Archilochus
to touch the nightingale &

feel those flashing feathers
                on my fingertips &
feel the fluttering wings
                upon my begging lips.

ἀηδονιδεύς

## COFFEE HOUSE PRESS

THE COFFEE HOUSES of seventeenth-century England were places of fellowship where ideas could be freely exchanged. In the cafés of Paris in the early years of the twentieth century, the surrealist, cubist, and dada art movements began. The coffee houses of 1950s America provided refuge and tremendous literary energy. Today, coffee house culture abounds at corner shops and online.

Coffee House Press continues these rich traditions. We envision all our authors and all our readers—be they in their living room chairs, at the beach, or in their beds—joining us around an ever-expandable table, drinking coffee and telling tales. And in the process of this exchange of stories by writers who speak from many communities and cultures, the American mosaic becomes reinvented, and reinvigorated.

We invite you to join us in our effort to welcome new readers to our table, and to the tales told in the pages of Coffee House Press books.

Please visit www.coffeehousepress.org
for more information.

# COLOPHON

*Thirsting for Peace in a Raging Century* was designed at Coffee House Press,
in the historic Grain Belt Brewery's Bottling House near downtown Minneapolis.
The text is set in Sabon.

# FUNDER ACKNOWLEDGMENTS

Coffee House Press is an independent nonprofit literary publisher. Our books are
made possible through the generous support of grants and gifts from many founda-
tions, corporate giving programs, state and federal support, and through donations
from individuals who believe in the transformational power of literature. Coffee
House receives major general operating support from the McKnight Foundation,
the Bush Foundation, from Target, and from the Minnesota State Arts Board,
through an appropriation by the Minnesota State Legislature and from the National
Endowment for the Arts. Coffee House also receives support from: three anony-
mous donors; Abraham Associates; the Elmer L. and Eleanor J. Andersen
Foundation; Allan Appel; Bill Berkson; the James L. and Nancy J. Bildner
Foundation; the Patrick and Aimee Butler Family Foundation; the Buuck Family
Foundation; the law firm of Fredrikson & Byron, PA.; Jennifer Haugh; Anselm
Hollo and Jane Dalrymple-Hollo; Jeffrey Hom; Stephen and Isabel Keating; Robert
and Margaret Kinney; the Kenneth Koch Literary Estate; Allan & Cinda Kornblum;
Seymour Kornblum and Gerry Lauter; the Lenfestey Family Foundation; Ethan J.
Litman; Mary McDermid; Rebecca Rand; Debby Reynolds; the law firm of
Schwegman, Lundberg, Woessner, PA.; Charles Steffey and Suzannah Martin; John
Sjoberg; Jeffrey Sugerman; Stu Wilson and Mel Barker; the Archie D. & Bertha H.
Walker Foundation; the Woessner Freeman Family Foundation; and many other
generous individual donors.

*This activity is made possible
in part by a grant from the
Minnesota State Arts Board,
through an appropriation by the
Minnesota State Legislature
and a grant from the National
Endowment for the Arts.*

NATIONAL
ENDOWMENT
FOR THE ARTS

MINNESOTA
STATE ARTS BOARD

TARGET.

To you and our many readers across the country,
we send our thanks for your continuing support.

*Good books are brewing at coffeehousepress.org*